DATING ETIQUETTE FOR *Singles*

A FAMILY LIFE HANDBOOK
VOLUME 1

MANNIE SAMUELSEN AZENDA

Dating Etiquette for Singles

The names, characters, places, and incidents portrayed in this book are fictitious. No identification with actual persons (living or dead) and places is intended or should be inferred.

Tellwell Talent
www.tellwell.ca

ISBN
978-0-2288-6056-3 (Hardcover)
978-0-2288-6055-6 (Paperback)
978-0-2288-6057-0 (eBook)

TABLE OF CONTENTS

DEDICATION

I dedicate this book to the loving memory of my dad, Samuel Azenda Abiagi, who mentored me and helped me become the person I am today. Dad, you taught me what it means to serve God. You also taught me the value of hard work, strong moral values, and humility. As well, I learned how to be a dad just by watching you. You truly were the epitome of an exemplary father.

Additionally, I dedicate this book to the evergreen memory of my mom, Hannah K. Azenda. Your insight, foresight, and wisdom remain unparalleled. I am grateful for your prayers that only a very special mom like you could have prayed. You were simply the best!

Finally, I dedicate this book to my grandma, Ruth Ashide Abiagi, the linchpin that held the family together. You worked tirelessly and sacrificed for the well-being of our family. Your entrepreneurial spirit and energy were second to none.

ACKNOWLEDGEMENTS

A special thanks to my wife and friend, Dr. Chino Azenda, for her dedication and relentless support in my life and ministry.

I owe my children a debt of gratitude for painstakingly going through the manuscript and providing invaluable feedback.

I am deeply grateful to the following important individuals who through careful review of the manuscript, prayer, encouragement, and support have contributed to this book's publication: Pastor Helen Burns, Hon. Stockwell Day, Ed and Carol Huculak, Toyin Odufeso, Mike Bolton, Stella Jonah, Chinwe Ahimie, Rosmond Adair, Dr. Johnson Rogho, Joe and Pat Nwaroh, Henry and Maureen Oluedo, Glory Shav, Vincent Fasegha and Moses Edjovi.

INTRODUCTION

As humans, we prepare for a lot of things in our lives. And rightly so! We prepare for important life events because it's the natural thing to do. For example, would a good student not prepare for an upcoming exam? Or why wouldn't an expectant mother prepare for the arrival of her baby? Or why wouldn't anyone give serious thought about and take steps to plan for their retirement? Or how many people would want to go on a family vacation and not take the time to prepare? In each of these situations, the overarching motivation for preparing is to make sure that we get it right the first time. It also means that we're acutely aware if we don't prepare we risk failing.

Of all the life events that we normally prepare for, marriage is the most significant phase of our lives that requires the greatest amount of effort. It is the most significant because, for most people, this will be the longest phase of their lives in terms of its duration. For example, someone who gets married at the age of thirty and lives to be eighty years old will have been married for fifty years of their life. Think about how sweet and fulfilling your life would be spending those fifty years in a blissful marriage. But the opposite is also true for anyone if they squander those precious fifty years of their life. Needless to say that an express path to committing that mistake simply is by not adequately preparing for marriage and how you'll spend those years.

In addition to not doing a great job in spending that prime phase of your life, you may not find true fulfillment in life overall. I've watched some people's lives become totally messed up because they got it all wrong with their marriage. Erroneously, some of those people felt that they could help themselves by divorcing and remarrying. Frequently, this strategy does not work for most people. There is an abundance of statistics and research demonstrating when the first marriage fails that any subsequent ones are even more likely to fail. But let's get this right: *the first wrong step is the failure to adequately prepare for the first marriage.* If sufficient intentional preparation was made, the first marriage wouldn't have failed and the need for the subsequent marriage would not have risen.

There could be an argument made in some quarters that people are dating for longer periods of time these days than they used to a few decades ago. That argument may be valid to some extent, but I'll suggest that it is not about how long the dating period lasts. It is about the depth of the intentionality of the couple involved.

Therefore, the burden God has placed on my heart is not to encourage people to date for longer periods of time. The burden is to address two key aspects of the process of preparing for marriage. **First, if you're already dating, how are you going about it?** In other words, are you being intentional about your dating experience? Have you crafted the goals for your dating experience? What do you intend to get out of the dating experience? If you have clearly defined the goals, how intentionally are you pursuing those goals? **Second, what's your understanding of marriage from a biblical perspective?** Do you know what the mind of God is about marriage? Do you understand what the Bible says about marriage? Do you know that marriage is meant for "adults" and not for "children"?

These are the key questions that this book has amply addressed. Majority of young people unconsciously know that they're going to marry at some point in their lives. However, any keen observer will agree that many singles are failing to appreciate the need to be intentional about their preparation for marriage. Thus, the inspiration I have received is to write about a solution that will fill that critical gap in the marriage process—preparation. The main perspective of this book is that good preparation is a recipe for success. Therefore, the inspiration behind this book is to help couples intending to marry to prepare for the marathon of a lifelong marriage.

Key Assumptions

I heartily welcome readers from all backgrounds and religious persuasions. I pray this book will be a blessing to every reader's life, and serve as an essential guide to help prepare you for marriage. However, I'd like to note that this book is written from an evangelical Christian perspective. As a result, I assume as a baseline understanding that the reader accepts the Bible as the highest authority in all matters of the Christian faith, and it is the ultimate guide to victorious living.

I assume the reader understands that the premise of this book is from the perspective that strengthening family life begins with an intentional courtship. It does not include life outside of the family context. This book is not a one-size-fits-all solution, which means this book focuses narrowly on what the Bible teaches about courtship in terms of a family setting only.

Finally, let me reiterate once again that this book will bless anyone who reads it. However, the inspiration I have received is to write a book that will be most beneficial to the following three main categories of people:

- You're single with a desire to please God in all that you do and are looking for the tools to improve your dating experience and ensure you date in the right way.
- You're a parent who's looking for a balanced and biblically based material to help guide your young adult children as they begin to date and prepare for marriage.
- You're involved in the field of marriage counselling, either as a pastor or as a lay leader in your church.

As I write this book, I am praying that everyone that reads it will exercise extra care as they read, and will renounce any mindset they have about marriage that may not be based on the word of God. I pray they will read it with an open and teachable heart. And lastly, I hope they will allow the Holy Spirit to minister to them like He has never done before.

If the foundations are destroyed,
What can the righteous do?

Psalms 11:3

CHAPTER ONE

BE READY FOR MARRIAGE

Dating usually is the starting point in relationships that will eventually evolve into marriage. It's the foundation of any marriage. It's difficult to overstate the importance of the foundation of anything—whether it's a relationship, a building structure, an organization, or an institution. A high-functioning marriage begins with a thoughtful courtship period. Therefore, getting the foundation right is essential for a relationship that'll go on to become a stable and blissful marriage.

Unfortunately, not many people are giving this all-important phase of marriage the attention that it deserves. As you'll see throughout this book, I recommend that singles who are dating to get married should clearly understand what marriage is. That understanding should be followed closely by paying attention to each other's personality and character. Similarly important is the need to understand each other's family, cultural, and spiritual backgrounds as much as possible. These are important topics to pay close attention to because they are the potential sources of many of the problems that may come up in your marriage.

Some singles have argued that the lessons of married life are best learned during marriage. Such singles often deem that they should be left alone. Some normally say things like this: We'll get married and learn as we go. To such people I will say, please learn all that you can about marriage now before you get married because you'll still have your hands full with things to learn as a newlywed. Some of the learnings will come as a big surprise to you. Therefore, it would be prudent for you to take the time to learn what can be best learned during courtship, and then learn the rest that you absolutely couldn't be taught during this period once you marry.

The Real Meaning of "Leave and Cleave"

When God gave Adam his wife, Adam responded by stating, "This is now bone of my bones And flesh of my flesh . . ." (Genesis 2:23 NKJV). God in turn, said that since woman was created out of man, that the man should leave his father and mother and cleave to his wife, and that the two should become one flesh (Genesis 2:24). This is the first occurrence of these two important words together in the Bible.

According to the online dictionary, <u>the word "leave" means to go away from a person, thing, or location</u>. <u>And "to cleave" means to glue firmly, loyally, and unwaveringly.</u> Therefore, a paraphrase of "leave and cleave" is that a man should leave his father and mother and "be glued firmly and unwaveringly" to his wife.

Adam's response tells us that he instantly recognized Eve as an integral part of himself. It seems clear that such recognition derives from the genetic affinity and emotions that he felt toward Eve. He knew without any doubt that Eve was created out of him, and he knew that Eve was one and the same as him. Adam said, *Now, this is bone of my bones and flesh of my flesh.*

Perhaps, if there had been other women besides Eve, Adam would still have picked Eve because he would have recognized her as the "right" woman for him. For that reason, I'll leverage this line of thought and the understanding of Adam's reaction to endorse the notion that for every Christian there is the "right" soulmate.

Further to this theme of being certain about your soulmate, I've often recommended that singles should refrain from the mindset that anyone can develop into that perfect someone. Such a mindset is a gamble. As I've spoken to dozens of singles about dating and marriage, I've met many young believers who normally ask whether it matters if the person they're in a relationship with is a Christian or not? Some have actually suggested that it doesn't really matter because after all, they would be capable of converting their partners once they were married.

I remember one zealous young lady who was exuberant enough to ask me if I had forgotten her zeal for the Lord so soon? She went on to try and assure me not to lose confidence in her as she would be able to get him seriously committed to God.

Unfortunately, young people who think like this young lady tend to forget that though their zeal is important, it's not nearly enough to convert a single soul to Christ. They fail to realize that it's not even within their power to convert anyone. Conversion of souls is entirely the work of the Holy Spirit.

Therefore, to meet the "right" person for you and to build a lifetime relationship with them, you need to believe that God will lead you to that person. He alone knows how to arrange that perfect encounter. For this reason, no one needs to fret over how to meet the right person.

The Minimum Qualifications

It isn't difficult to know who the "right" person is for a lifetime partner. The Bible gives us the fundamental attribute of the Christian identity as an important clue. In Paul's second letter to the Corinthians, he warned them not to be unequally yoked with unbelievers. In that same epistle, he asked them what agreement has light with darkness or the temple of God with Belial? (2 Corinthians 6:14-17).

He then commanded them to remain separated from unbelievers. Paul's timeless message must remain our baseline even today. Expressed simply, the baseline requirement for the "right" person is that the person must be a Christian. That means that no matter who he or she is, if they aren't a Christian, it's a non-starter.

The subject of being unequally yoked with someone is a major issue for many singles in our contemporary context. This is true both for young and mature singles. I'll emphasize that if your Christian faith is important to you, then don't contemplate starting a relationship with someone whose faith you aren't sure of. Getting into a serious relationship with somebody whose Christian conviction you're unsure of is not wise.

Going into such relationships can sometimes be as costly as having to choose between remaining a committed Christian and remaining married. Sadly, I know of a few of such situations. Don't be fooled by the euphoria of the initial stages of the relationship. It's important not to forget that it's going to be a lifelong relationship that must outlive the initial excitement people feel when they first fall in love.

Many singles who are in love sometimes are very simplistic and even overconfident by believing that they'll make both the spiritual and marital aspects of their relationship work. I've seen both men and women exhibit this type of overconfidence.

Regrettably, I've come across many singles who have fallen for the same lie made by their dates. Their date tells them that they're a believer, but they don't watch closely enough to get the assurance that the person is indeed who they say they are. I agree that in general, it isn't up to you to seek proof from people who say that they are a Christian. However, I strongly believe that it is up to you to seek proof of the Christian identity from someone whom you are going to marry. No one should ever lose sight of the fact that once you marry them, you'll become "one flesh" with them. That fact should not be taken for granted by anyone. Taking it for granted means that half of you'll be for the Lord and the other half will be for something else.

> *No one should ever lose sight of the fact that once you marry somebody, you'll become "one flesh" with that person.*

It's a tedious undertaking to try to spoon-feed or babysit a spouse into becoming a committed Christian. Beware of the second law of thermodynamics, which states that heat flows spontaneously from a hot to a cold body. By way of illustration, this law tells us that an ice cube must melt on a hot day rather than becoming colder. I find that this law applies to spiritual matters as well.

In a relationship such as marriage, a Christian who is fervent is going to lose much of their fervency until they level out with their spiritually lukewarm spouse. And if care is not taken, they'll both fall away from the faith. Therefore, be careful not to make the mistake of saying that you'll get him or her to become a committed Christian. While that might be possible, there is a significant chance you may not be successful. You run the risk of being dragged down spiritually by your spouse.

> *It's a tedious undertaking to try to spoon-feed or babysit a spouse into becoming a committed Christian.*

For these reasons, I'll add that it is much better if both individuals are closely aligned in their faith as well as doctrinal orientation. For instance, Mikayla a fervent young lady not more than thirty years old, once told me of her ordeal with her former husband. Mikayla committed her life to the Lord in her late teen years at a Christian summer camp. When she was in her early twenties she met Jake, her would-be husband, a nominal Christian who had no assurance of salvation nor a personal relationship with the Lord. According to her, Jake only went to church when he felt bored or had nothing else to do.

Jake and Mikayla dated for about two years. Throughout that period they didn't have a focused discussion about the apparent difference between their levels of commitment to the Lord. I asked Mikayla, "Why didn't you bring up the difference in your views about the need for more commitment to the Lord with Jake?"

She disclosed her naivety to me. She said, "There were three main reasons. The first was that I took for granted that I'd be able to help Jake become dedicated to God. The second reason was that I loved him very much and didn't want to raise anything that appeared controversial or made Jake uncomfortable. The third was that Jake didn't object to my commitment to going to church or any other Christian activity, so I felt there was no compelling reason to bring it up for discussion. Neither did he question my Christian views while the dating period lasted."

They got married, and occasionally, Mikayla would skip church on Sunday. This usually happened whenever Jake declined to attend church with her. This inconsistency in attending church continued but with increasing frequency over the first three years of their marriage.

By the fourth year of their marriage, Mikayla repented and started living out her faith in a more active and compelling way. She would demand that it was important they both go to church together every week with their two young children. According to Mikayla, Jake's response to her demand was that her new attitude about church was slowly but surely encroaching into his inner peace. He complained that he was feeling judged by Mikayla.

Jake also told her on more than one occasion that he didn't want her to shove religion down the throat of his children. He stated that it was his resolve for Mikayla to allow his children to grow up and find God themselves. Mikayla further disclosed that the tension started building up in their marriage as weeks and months passed. She told me that Jake openly showed dislike and even disdain for her views in other areas of their family life.

By their fifth wedding anniversary, the conflict between them had grown to become out of control. Consequently, on one particular occasion Jake directly threatened her by stating, "Look, Mikayla, at this point, I must invite you to minimize your newly found religious fanaticism, or the end of our marriage will be inevitable." It was a tough choice for Mikayla to make, especially in view of their two young children, but she eventually opted to keep what Jake called her religious fanaticism. They mutually agreed that Jake would take custody of their children.

I believe that such a situation could have been avoided if she had been able to turn Jake into a dedicated evangelistic believer like herself, which Mikayla probably assumed she could do prior to getting married. Or if, for the sake of their marriage and children, she could have sadly joined Jake and become an occasional church-going person. Mikayla's story is just one example among many that highlights the importance of ensuring that you have a well-aligned doctrinal background with your prospective spouse.

I would like to share a few more thoughts about meeting that right person. It's safe to commit your desire to meet that "right" person into God's hands the same way you do in all other areas of your life. How could you trust God to care about giving you the desires of your heart, yet doubt that he's able or not believe he cares about the most important human relationship of your life?

Marriage is both a physical and spiritual undertaking. Therefore, any attempt to separate or dissolve a marriage causes multi-faceted damage that can be manifested spiritually, financially, emotionally, and physically. And as you will see in *Volume 2*, Part Five, "The Anatomy of a Failed Marriage" the impact of divorce is usually felt far beyond the couple. It has a proven negative impact on the extended family as well as on society.

It is due to the great damage divorce is most likely to cause that the Lord stressed that it should be avoided. He firmly said that what God has joined together let no one put asunder (Mark 19:6). For emphasis, it should be noted that these are Jesus' words, who is the Author and Finisher of our faith.

A healthy and high-functioning marriage is God's desire for all of us. A healthy marriage begins with a thoughtful dating experience. What is a healthy marriage is detailed in the second book of my Family Life series, *The High-Functioning Marriage, Volume 2*. I'll assert that it isn't particularly difficult to identify a healthy marriage because a healthy marriage is practical and observable.

Thus, in the next chapters we will discuss some important points that'll help singles who intend to get married. I will provide important tools that'll help them through their courtship period and ultimately set the right tone for their lifelong marriage.

KEY TAKE AWAY

- Begin with an intentional and purposeful courtship period to become ready for a high-functioning marriage.
- Learn all that you can during the courtship period. Don't put off any learning opportunities.
- Take the time to understand the meaning of marriage and why God instituted it.
- Insist on dating a fellow Christian if you're a Christian. Otherwise, you'll be engaging in an unequal yoking, and that can be risky.
- Don't marry an unbeliever with the hope that you'll lead them to the Lord. Regardless of how genuine your intentions might be it is not advisable to date an unbeliever because you may not achieve your desired result.
- Believe that God will lead you to that right person he has ordained to be your spouse.

CHAPTER TWO

PREPARE FOR MARRIAGE

A good friend of mine recently told me that the average engaged person in North America spends about twelve hours per week planning their wedding. Since a typical engagement lasts several months before the wedding, it's safe to estimate that the average person spends hundreds of hours planning their wedding day. Unfortunately, the same average person spends little to no time to plan for the rest of their lives following the wedding. Think about that for a moment!

It's also true that most people enjoy their wedding day, and it's not difficult to understand why. They've spent a lot of time planning how to host a great wedding and make it special, and they executed the event based on the plans they made throughout those hundreds of hours of preparation.

It's in our human nature to prepare for things that are important to us. For example, a mother who is expecting a baby keeps her expected delivery date in view as she gets ready for the arrival of her baby. We prepare for job interviews. Students prepare for exams. We also prepare for important trips and pack based on the preparations and plans we've made.

Just imagine what would happen if there was no adequate preparation made in any of the above examples. Certainly, the outcome wouldn't be very pleasant. Therefore, we must take to heart the adage that if one fails to prepare, the person prepares to fail. Isn't that so true?

You must have heard people say that marriage is for mature adults, and it's also a fact that it takes some maturing to fully appreciate the importance of getting ready for any important life endeavour. For that reason, no one should contemplate going into a marriage until he or she is ready. Otherwise, you may go into marriage only to make a failure of it.

> *No one should contemplate going into a marriage until he or she is ready for it.*

Properly Understanding Marriage

The first step toward readiness is to take the time to understand the true meaning of marriage. Does understanding the meaning of marriage sound superfluous to you? It shouldn't! Understanding the meaning of marriage may sound too obvious, but it's the necessary first step to help you realize the importance of marriage.

I've taken the liberty to stress this point because marriage means different things to different people these days. For some people, it's about any two people who like each other calling family and friends and going to a marriage registry for a ceremony. Considering the diversity of these viewpoints, I have aligned myself with Dr. Wolfinger's belief, that proper education about the institution of marriage has become more urgent than ever before.

> *The Bible is the reference manual and final authority for anyone seeking to know the heart of God regarding marriage and every endeavour in life.*

In the book of Matthew, we have this account of Jesus' encounter with the Pharisees:

The Pharisees also came to Him, testing Him, and saying to Him, "Is it lawful for a man to divorce his wife for just any reason?" And He answered and said to them, "Have you not read that He who made them at the beginning 'made them male and female,' and said, 'For this reason a man shall leave his father and mother and be joined to his wife, and the two shall become one flesh? So then, they are no longer two but one flesh'? Therefore, what God has joined together, let not man separate." They said to Him, "Why then did Moses command to give a certificate of divorce, and to put her away?" He said to them, "Moses, because of the hardness of your hearts, permitted you to divorce your wives, but from the beginning it was not so." (Matthew 19:3–8 NKJV)

This passage shines a bright light onto what marriage is. I've underlined some phrases in the passage above that I believe will guide us to gain a better understanding of the message. The Lord Jesus said here that it's God who has joined the couple in marriage. That means that marriage is more than a pastor or a marriage commissioner leading the new couple through the marriage vows at a ceremony.

"Have you not read that He who made them at the beginning 'made them male and female,' . . ." (v. 4) underscores the fact that according to our Lord Jesus, marriage is between a man and a woman.

In verse 6, Jesus says, "what God has joined together . . ." and that simply means that God must be recognized as the one who divinely joins the couple in holy matrimony. Therefore, those who are already married and those who are contemplating getting married should recognize that it's this irreplaceable role of God in marriage that makes it such a hallowed institution.

Jesus continues by saying, "let not man separate . . ." (v. 6), which succinctly answers the important question about divorce. Divorce was not part of the original design God had for the institution of marriage. Couples were supposed to be married and stay married for a lifetime. But as time progressed, due to a diversity of reasons, men started seeking to divorce their wives. Jesus told the Pharisees who came to him with a question regarding this matter that Moses permitted them to divorce their wives only because of the hardness of their hearts (v. 8a). Perhaps, they persistently went to Moses asking him to grant them the option to divorce their wives, and out of weariness Moses permitted them to put aside their wives.

Jesus told the Pharisees that in the beginning, it was not so (v. 8b). "In the beginning" refers to the time when God determined that it was not good for Adam to be alone and proceeded to make a wife for him. The desire for divorce, like all other unpleasant human experiences, has its roots in the fall of man that distorted God's perfect creation. (See Genesis 3).

Christ's teaching in this passage suggests that divorce is a practice that exists in a realm where those involved insist on having their way regardless of what God thinks. Of course, I'm aware of many divorce situations where there's only one spouse that wants it at all costs regardless of available interventions. I have much more to say about divorce in *Volume 2* of my *Family Life Handbook* series in Part Five, "The Anatomy of a Failed Marriage."

Self-Awareness

The second step toward being ready for marriage is for the couple to take the time to understand their unique individuality. There are several skills that lead to success in life and self-awareness is one of them, although it is often not seen by many as a critical trait. We need this skill at various stages and in endeavours of life including, but not limited to self-management, career management, relationship management, financial management, and so on. However, understanding who we are, how we think, and how we operate is vital to knowing who we are and who God has made us to be. The couple should be able to make an accurate assessment of their own personality, strengths, and weaknesses.

> *We need self-awareness at various stages and in endeavours of life including but not limited to self-management, career management, relationship management, financial management, and so on.*

There is a fitting quote by Ann Landers that goes like this: "Know yourself. Don't accept your dog's admiration as conclusive evidence that you are wonderful." Your dog is not necessarily the best person to let you know what a wonderful person you are. Do a careful self-study and learn who you really are.

From the ancient Greek Aphorism "know thyself" to western psychology, the topic of self-awareness has been studied by philosophers and psychologists for much of the twentieth century. Daniel Goleman, a registered psychologist, proposed a popular definition of self-awareness in his best-selling book *Emotional Intelligence* as, knowing one's internal states, preferences, resources, and intuitions. It's safe to say that Goleman's definition places emphasis on the ability to monitor our inner world, thoughts, and emotions as they arise.

> *Know yourself. Don't accept your dog's admiration as conclusive evidence that you are wonderful.*
>
> *-Ann Landers*

According to Mr. Goleman, self-awareness is the foundation and cornerstone of emotional intelligence, which is the ability to monitor our emotions and thoughts from moment to moment. This ability is key to understanding ourselves better, being at peace with who we are, and proactively managing our thoughts, emotions, and behaviours. Our emotional intelligence hinges on how well we know ourselves.

Two other psychologists Shelley Duvall and Robert Wicklund also developed a theory of self-awareness. The duo proposed the following: when we focus our attention on ourselves, we evaluate and compare our current behaviour to our internal standards and values. We become self-conscious as objective evaluators of ourselves.

> *Self-awareness is the foundation and cornerstone to emotional intelligence.*
>
> *-Daniel Goleman*

Unfortunately, not many people can confidently say that they know themselves. It's this ignorance that impedes people's ability to build and sustain long-lasting relationships. Therefore, self-awareness is an essential determinant that can help you have a successful family life and help with all other aspects of your life as well.

> *Therefore, self-awareness is an essential determinant that can help you lead a successful family life and help with all other aspects of your life.*

How to Cultivate Self-Awareness

You shouldn't be discouraged because you don't yet know who you are. Like it is the case in all areas of our lives, you can learn and grow in your self-awareness. But you may need some tools to help you grow. Here're some suggestions to guide you:

Ask God to help you know yourself

This is the most important step to take as you embark on the journey to become self-aware. God who is our maker is all-knowing, so he knows us very intimately. You can pray like King David prayed, "Search me, O God, and know my heart; Try me, and know my anxieties; And see if there is any wicked way in me, And lead me in the way everlasting." (Psalm 139:23-24 NKJV)

Let the Bible be your mirror

According to the Guinness World Records as of 1995, the Bible is the best-selling book of all time with an estimated 5 billion copies sold and distributed. The fact that such a large number of the Bible have been sold worldwide shouldn't surprise anyone, and there's a multitude of very good reasons. It wouldn't be an exaggeration to suggest that the Bible has an answer for every human need or situation. No other book exists that can make such claim. It also describes the condition of every human heart and personality. That's why the Bible is qualified to be your mirror; it can reflect who you are, why you think the way you do, as well as explain why you behave in the manner that you act. The Bible is the discerner of the thoughts and intents of the heart as it states, "For the word of God is living and powerful, and sharper than any two-edged sword, piercing even to the division of soul and spirit, and of joints and marrow, and is a discerner of the thoughts and intents of the heart." (Hebrews 4:12 NKJV).

Scrutinize your thoughts

As humans we're constantly thinking. The way we think reveals who we are. We learned from the book of Proverbs that as a man thinks, so is he (Proverbs 23:7). Perhaps the only time we take a break from thinking is when we're asleep. In fact, right now you're thinking even as you read this section of this book. Your thought process will greatly help you on your journey to cultivate self-awareness. It's part of the reason why the Bible says that we should guard our heart with all diligence for out of it are the issues of life. (Proverbs 4:23).

Listen to yourself

Beside monitoring what your thoughts are, it's also important to be the audience of what comes out of your mouth. Pay close attention to what you say because the pattern of what you say reveals who you are. The Bible says that out of the abundance of the heart the mouth speaks (Matthew 12:34). What do you talk about? You likely have been part of a gathering where one individual does all the talking and it is all about themselves. In this situation, everyone will be asking if the speaker is ever going to stop? Don't they realize they have been talking non-stop about themselves the whole time? Such behaviour is a glaring display of the lack of self-awareness.

Keep a journal

Writing not only helps us process our thoughts, but it also makes us feel connected and at peace with ourselves. Writing can create more head space as you let your thoughts flow out onto paper. I can confirm that writing down things we are grateful for helps to increase happiness and satisfaction. You can also use the journal to record about your inner state. Try this at home. Choose a half day on a weekend and pay close attention to your inner world—what you're feeling, what you're saying to yourself—and make a note of what you observe every hour. You may be surprised by what you'd write down!

Know Your Marital Responsibilities

The third step toward becoming marriage-ready is that you understand and determine in your heart that you can live up to the marital responsibilities. I have described these in great details in *Volume 2* of *A Family Life Handbook* series.

Grow into Maturity

The fourth step toward becoming marriage-ready is for the couple to make sure that they have grown and matured into adulthood. As marriage is both a physical and spiritual undertaking, the required maturity must be both in terms of the physical and spiritual.

Being physically mature doesn't mean that a couple should be forty years old or a specific age before being considered mature to marry. Maturity is measured more by the character development of an individual. I've seen some adults in their forties behave as if they were teenagers. Physical maturity can be seen in how an individual approaches issues, their sense of judgment, and even their value system that they've developed over the years. It also includes how they react to or manage difficult situations. All these things will evolve and change as we grow and mature.

> *Maturity is measured by the character development of an individual.*

The book of Hebrews aptly captures the state of spiritual immaturity this way:

> *For though by this time you ought to be teachers, you need someone to teach you again the first principles of the oracles of God; and you have come to need milk and not solid food. For everyone who partakes only of milk is unskilled in the word of righteousness, for he is a babe. But solid food belongs to those who are of full age, that is, those who by reason of use have their senses exercised to discern both good and evil. (Hebrews 5:12–14 (NKJV)*

This passage provides a mirror for believers to check themselves and see where they stack up on the spiritual maturity scale. Keeping in mind the things the author of the book of Hebrews has listed in Hebrews 6:1-3 as the principles of the doctrine of Christ, here are some questions that will guide you in knowing how you measure:

- Are you still in need of someone to encourage or teach you how to ***pray*** on your own?
- Are you still in need of someone who will tell you that you need to have a ***Bible study*** routine?
- Are you still needing to be told that ***regular church attendance*** is vital for your spiritual growth?
- Are you still looking for someone to teach you how to ***give*** your ***time***, ***talent***, and ***money*** toward the work of God?
- Are you still needing to be taught about **water baptism**?
- Are you lacking a good understanding of the ***ministry of the Holy Spirit*** in your personal life as a Christian?
- Do you know why you absolutely need the ***baptism of the Holy Spirit***?

The above passage also tells us that we don't only need to know these things, but as mature Christians, we should be in a position to teach others why the principles are crucial in the spiritual growth of a believer. When you are confident with your understanding of these "first principles of the oracles of God" and are able and willing to teach others, then it demonstrates that you are growing and maturing. It also shows that you will become increasingly hungry for more "solid food." Therefore, it's important for the couple to strive to become mature because not only will it be excellent for their personal lives, but it will nicely impact their marriage as well.

An easy way of measuring one's maturity level is to exhibit some capability to be a mentor, teacher, or someone others can look up to. As the husband is the family's immediate pastor or spiritual leader, he'll need to do much more work to attain a clear state of maturity—both on a physical and spiritual level. I say this because expectedly, most women will look up to their husbands for leadership in every area of their family life. For that reason, there's usually a huge sense of disappointment when that leadership is found to be lacking from the husband. Therefore, husbands must make every effort to grow, mature, and become that confident leader that provides effective guidance to his family.

To be spiritually mature, you must be born again. Jesus answered Nicodemus' question in John 3:3, Verily, verily, I say to you, except a man be born again, he cannot see the kingdom of God. Perhaps you're already married, or are in a relationship and working toward getting married, and you aren't yet born again. It's not too late. You can do it today, even right now as you read this book. Without salvation, you cannot talk about spiritual maturity. In fact, without salvation, one won't even fathom what spiritual maturity is all about.

Perhaps you are already married or are in a relationship and working toward getting married, and you aren't yet born again. It is not too late. You can do it today, even right now as you read this book.

The book of Romans provides a blueprint of how to be born again, and it says:

That if you confess with your mouth the Lord Jesus and believe in your heart that God has raised Him from the dead, you will be saved. For with the heart one believes unto righteousness, and with the mouth confession is made unto salvation. For the Scripture says, "Whoever believes on Him will not be put to shame." (Romans 10:9-11 NKJV)

Being born again is the critical first step, and it is akin to taking a step to enter a large house through the main door. Gaining entrance into a house but remaining only at the entrance isn't good enough. After gaining entrance into a house, you'll need to proceed to explore what's available inside the house.

Therefore, don't just stop at the crucial first step of confessing Jesus as Lord and Saviour. You should endeavour to go further because there's still a lot that needs to be explored and enjoyed in your new relationship with Jesus. To grow spiritually, start learning how to pray on a regular basis. Accompany your prayer life with reading and studying the word of God.

As soon as possible, seek and receive the baptism of the Holy Spirit. Christian living is a marathon race, not a sprint, and to run successfully over the long haul you will need lots of help from the Holy Spirit. With Him, the spiritual marathon becomes a lot more interesting and exciting.

The next step that you must not miss is to discover the riches that are available to you in your relationship with Jesus. An excellent guide for grasping the benefits of your relationship with Jesus is my previous book, *The Greatest Exchange*. A Christian who will go far in the journey of faith must rely on the ministry of the Holy Spirit.

> *A Christian who will go far in the journey of faith must rely on the ministry of the Holy Spirit.*

Financial Readiness

The Bible says in Ecclesiastes 10:19 that money answers all things. That passage underscores the importance of money. I'm not going to do a detailed study about the importance of money here as it's outside the scope of this book. However, a good reference on this subject is found in Chapter Eight of my previous book *The Greatest Exchange*.

Anyone who's married knows that marriage comes with additional responsibilities. An important part of those additional responsibilities is related to finance. For example, the couple will have to fund their premarital expenses, the wedding ceremony, the honeymoon, a suitable home, and so on. Therefore, it'll take a decent amount of financial literacy and maturity to manage all the ongoing expenses effectively. As Linda Waite and Maggie Gallagher eloquently stated in their book *A Case for Marriage*, a married couple will grow their wealth and actually become affluent.

In one of my recent workshops on dating, someone asked me what financial maturity actually meant. She wanted to know if it meant the size of one's paycheque or bank account. My answer is quite simple: it has little to do with how much one earns or how much money someone has in their bank account. What is important is that the man has a stable source of income before he considers getting married. It'll be entirely up to the couple to decide if a husband's minimum wage earnings will be sufficient to sustain them or not.

In God's design, as Apostle Paul recorded in Ephesians 5:23–24, "For the husband is head of the wife, as also Christ is head of the church; and He is the Saviour of the body. Therefore, just as the church is subject to Christ, so let the wives be to their own husbands in everything."

Two income households have become the norm these days. However, based on this biblical provision, an aspiring husband needs to be financially prepared with a stable financial income to fulfill that headship role effectively. If the wife is also an income earner, which is becoming increasingly normal these days that will be a welcomed bonus. The wife's secondary income will come in handy in a situation where her husband takes time off to acquire further education, loses his job, or he temporarily is without an income for any other reason.

My emphasis on what the Bible says about the husband being the head of their family doesn't in any way suggest that women are not capable, neither is it to demean the incredible capabilities that women possess. It would be a display of ignorance for anyone to attempt to undermine the obvious abilities of women because they are capable in every way! For example, the world has seen female prime ministers, presidents, parliamentarians, military generals, chief executive officers of major corporations, world class evangelists, heads of large ministries, and so on. Some female astronauts have successfully gone to space and back. Women are quite capable of doing amazing things if given the opportunity.

> *The world has seen female prime ministers, presidents, parliamentarians, chief executive officers of major corporations, evangelists, heads of large ministries, and so on. Some female astronauts have successfully gone to space and back.*

However, I was curious to learn from many of my female confidants that many women feel out of place when faced with the responsibility of being the main provider in an intact marriage. Of course, by their disclosure they aren't saying that all women lack the ability of being the breadwinners in their families. I've seen some who have done so quite well. But according to those female confidants, somehow not all women are able to bring themselves mentally and psychologically to effectively take on that responsibility of fending for the whole family, especially when it must be on a permanent basis. In fact, some have suggested that it just doesn't feel right for them to play that role.

One of my female colleagues once said something that I found very interesting regarding this topic. A few years ago, our company was going through a major reorganization. As a result, the existing organizational structure was dissolved, and we were asked to apply for available positions. On this particular day that my colleague and I were chatting, I asked her which of the management roles she was going to apply for. Her response was, "Not me! I'm a secondary income earner, so I won't bother applying for any of those leadership positions. Let me leave the men who are the primary earners for their families to take on such roles." Obviously, not all women think like that, but there's probably a sizable percentage of them who do feel this way.

Financial maturity includes the ability to make well-thought-out financial decisions and choices. It would be a good idea to take a formal financial management course. The course should help with how to prioritize financial options, prepare monthly budgets, and be mature and disciplined enough to stick to that budget. For example, it doesn't show any sign of financial maturity to take an exotic vacation when there's no money in the bank to pay next month's rent or mortgage.

> *Based on this biblical provision, it's important that the man has a stable financial income to fulfill that headship role effectively.*

Some Ways to Measure Financial Maturity[1]

Financial maturity is something that is demonstrable as well as measurable. It can be seen in the choices that you make. Being financially reckless is a behaviour that any married person should avoid, but particularly men who are often the main income earner for their family. I have provided below some observable characteristics of financially mature people. And depending on where you're on the maturity scale, these characteristics may be a guide for you to further pursue greater financial maturity and astuteness.

They don't live above their earnings

It is not a coincidence that I am placing this right at the top of the list of attributes of financially astute people. We all know that it's far easier to spend than it is to earn. For example, someone can go online in the comfort of their home and within minutes have easily spent $10,000. But it may take an average worker a few months to earn a net income of $10,000. Therefore, if you develop your financial management skills that'll help to keep your spending within the limits of your earnings, you'll be doing well.

Here are two important ways you can make sure that you're spending within the limits of your earnings.

Budget your money

It takes discipline to master the culture of budgeting. This includes how to *create* a budget and making sure that you *stick* to it. As you develop the budgeting habit, it's important to learn some tricks that will help you to resist the inevitable temptations to set your budget aside and spend frivolously. The simple concept of budgeting recognizes that you've a finite amount of money to spend within a specified timeframe. For example, your net income every two weeks may be $2,000. Your budget will help ensure that you're not going to spend more than $2,000 until the next pay hits your account. You also know that if you spend more than $2,000, which is your net earnings per pay period, you'll effectively be borrowing from your next pay period. If you still go ahead and spend more than $2,000, you don't need an oracle to advise you on where you're heading with your finances.

> *If you still go ahead and spend more than $2,000, you don't need an oracle to advise you on where you're heading with your finances.*

Use credit wisely

The Bible tells us that the borrower is a slave to the lender (Proverbs 22:7). In many cases, credit cards are a necessary evil. Most of us carry them to facilitate certain financial transactions where cash or debit may not be an option to complete a financial transaction. For example, you can't book a flight with your debit card no matter how much money you have in your account. Therefore, credit cards are sometimes both handy and necessary. However, as a rule of thumb you must learn to use available credit wisely. It is not very wise to routinely spend more than your net earnings and supplement it with your credit card.

The eighteen-year-old son of a family friend had an interesting experience with his credit card, and he learned the lesson from it the hard way. He was a freshman in university. As is the tradition of financial institutions during orientation week, they lined up their offers to woo students to sign up for their credit card.

This young man quickly was signed up for a credit card with a $10,000 limit on it, and began to spend like there was no tomorrow. As usual, the bank was diligent in sending him statements every month, but because he didn't understand what the credit card statements said and didn't know how to service his credit, he just threw away the statements. Meanwhile, he continued to spend using the credit card. After six months, he had no available room left on the card and had not paid anything toward the outstanding balance. He began receiving warnings that he was behind several months on making his minimum payments and that he should call to make payment arrangements. Finally, he decided to ask his mom what the warning letter meant. After his parents took the time to explain to him what he had got himself into he exclaimed that "credit cards were evil" and said that he'd never have anything to do with them again.

They're usually on top of their expenses

Small and big expenses can add up quite fast. Look for opportunities to reduce your expenses no matter how small. One deception about small expenses is that individually they appear to be inconsequential. But you must appreciate how much collectively they impact your bottom line; because, in the end you'll be contending with the aggregate of those small and big expenses. For instance, depending on the season you can turn down or off the heating or air conditioning when you leave the house. Or you can turn off the lights when no one is home, or turn them off in a room that is not occupied. You may also choose to use a refillable water bottle instead of buying a new case every week.

They mostly eat home-cooked meals

Eating out can be a good thing because of its convenience. You may have the opportunity to try new foods while spending time with family and friends. But the one obvious disadvantage is the cost differential between home-cooked meals and eating out. That differential can be huge sometimes. Obviously, no formal analysis is necessary to unearth that difference. Simply add up the cost of cooking at home versus eating out or ordering in food, and you'll know that in the interest of financial prudence which option will ultimately contribute to your financial independence over the long-term. You'll soon see how it makes a lot of sense to choose cooking at home majority of the time.

One way of keeping a tab on this ongoing expense is by budgeting. For example, an average eat-out meal costs $25 including taxes. When you add on a conservative $5 tip, that brings the total to $30. Assume you eat out thirty times in a month. That will bring the cost to $900 just for eating out. If your net earnings for a month is $4,000, it means that you're spending approximately one-quarter of your net earnings just on eating out. Keep in mind that this amount doesn't include your two other meals each day. You might view that $30 per meal looks small and you can easily afford this expense. But with the knowledge of the whole picture, it won't be difficult to see how much of your earnings is being spent in ways that can be conveniently avoided.

They think before spending their money

Financially mature people think hard and long before they spend their money. And there is a lot of wisdom in taking the time to do that thinking. Why would you work hard to earn your money and then spend it without careful thought? The benefit of thinking wisely before spending your money is to be able to answer the question of whether I really do need the item at this time or if I simply want it? Yes, in order to manage your money wisely, you must convince yourself that spending your money for that purpose is a sensible thing to do at that particular time. Haven't you ever wondered, "What was I thinking" about something you once purchased? You can minimize the frequency of asking yourself that question if every purchase you make is preceded by some careful thinking.

They don't buy just because it's on sale

You shouldn't buy something just because there's a huge discount on it. Only buy something that you really love and need. What's the point buying something simply because of the price if you'll never use it? An old episode of the *I Love Lucy* show poked fun at this common mistake. Lucy chided her friend for buying a 50-pound bag of dog food. Her friend defended herself by saying that it was half price. To which Lucy hilariously replied, "You don't have a dog!" If you find yourself thinking, "These shoes are 50 percent off and they're not that bad," take the money and buy a pair of shoes you actually like that are being sold at full price. You're more likely to get some use out of them.

They don't buy anything without first asking the price

Chuck went shopping with Sue, his girlfriend, for the first time since they started dating a few months ago. In their community the practice was not to put a price tag on the products in the store. To make a purchase, you must ask the shopkeeper how much the item that you want to buy costs. The nice thing about this practice is that you almost always have the opportunity to bargain to get a good price. At this time, Sue was not financially mature and she also came from a background that believed it was a show of class to buy things without bargaining.

Chuck was more experienced and financially prudent. He wanted to buy a pair of shoes for Sue. They entered a shoe store, and after he picked out a pair of shoes he asked how much it was being sold. The shopkeeper told him the price and Chuck started bargaining. Sue became very uncomfortable and even agitated by the process. In the end, Chuck and the storekeeper couldn't come to an agreement on the price. Chuck and Sue left the store and after a while entered another shoe store. Chuck saw another beautiful pair of shoes and asked for the price. He was told the price and again started bargaining. Sue really loved this particular pair of shoes and felt they were a perfect fit for her. For Chuck, he felt he had reached a good bargain. Chuck paid and their shopping was completed for that day.

As they were driving home Sue said to Chuck, "You are a tough deal finder, aren't you?"

"Am I?" Chuck turned and smiled at Sue while stating, "I try to be." Chuck didn't realize that it wasn't meant as a genuine complement, and that he was being mocked by Sue.

"But I was thoroughly embarrassed by your hard nose bargaining that you were doing," she told Chuck. "I am sorry to let you know, but, for me when I am shopping, I just pay whatever price they mention instead of embarrassing myself by bargaining." She continued, "To be completely honest with you I don't think I'll be at ease going shopping with you again. I don't want anyone thinking that I am poor."

Chuck asked her, "Does that means you're not happy that we got a good discount for these beautiful shoes that are also a perfect fit for you?" He added, "I strongly believe in bargaining, as it's the only way to know that you aren't being gouged."

Unfortunately, in terms of financial astuteness, Sue's thinking was pitiably backward. She failed to realize that poor was what she'd be if she continued with that sort of attitude.

> *For me, when I am shopping, I just pay whatever price they mention instead of embarrassing myself by bargaining.*

They avoid being "penny wise and a pound foolish"

This saying simply means that while you might be trying to save money on a minor expense, it could potentially mean you'll have to pay a much bigger expense later. For example, you may postpone changing the engine oil and keep driving your car until the engine is damaged. If this happens, you will have no other choice but to replace the engine or even might have to buy a new car. Getting your teeth cleaned regularly may not be a very pleasant experience, but if you don't do it, you may be setting yourself up for a root canal in the future. Therefore, the rule of thumb in good financial management is that you trim from the fat and not the essentials. To hold back when it comes to spending on the essentials of your daily life does not make good financial sense. You'll regret it if you do.

They avoid get-rich-quick schemes

There's hardly any such thing as get-rich-quick when it comes to thoughtful and transparent investing. Those who market such schemes know their target audience are people who need to grow up. Sustainable wealth comes through careful planning, typically over a long period of time. Think about it for a minute. When people do strike the proverbial gold, they probably don't go announcing it to the whole world.

Several years ago, I came across a fellow who crafted a get-rich-quick scheme in a city where I was living at the time. The philosophy behind the scheme was simply to collect deposits from people to pay to others. The maturity period for a deposit was only six months, during which, according to the architect of the scheme should yield a return of 100 percent. For example, if somebody deposited \$1,000 the same person would get \$2,000 after six months. All this scheme was intended to do was basically collect deposits and pay those whose deposits had matured. Most people who invested in the scheme were fully convinced that their lifetime opportunity to get rich had finally come. To maximize the return, many of the investors took out bank loans, while others sold their homes and invested in the scheme. Sadly, it was not long before the whole thing fell apart. After the collapse of the scheme, not a few people died of heart attacks.

The key to avoid being a victim of the get-rich-quick scheme is to have a financial plan. If you know enough to have a plan, then you'll also know that there's no such thing as getting rich quickly. This is consistent with what the Bible says: "The plans of the diligent lead surely to plenty, but those of everyone who is hasty, surely to poverty." (Proverbs 21:5 NKJV).

> *If you know enough to have a plan, then you'll also know that there's no such thing as getting rich quickly.*

They are driven by their financial goals

Without a clear goal and a doable plan, people tend to stay right where they are. Good goals illuminate the path between where you are and where you want to be. It's important to carefully set financial goals and priorities, and to be disciplined enough to stick to them. The Bible says, "Prepare your outside work, Make it fit for yourself in the field; And afterward build your house." (Proverbs 24:27 NKJV).

They regularly pay into a savings account or emergency fund

Regularly paying money into a savings account to be ready should an unexpected happen is a good habit that financially mature people often exhibit. But a savings account doesn't have to be used just to service an unexpected or negative event. Someone may say but I have faith, so nothing unexpected will happen to me. Putting money aside on a regular basis shows good planning and foresight. For example, you can use money from your savings account to renovate your kitchen or bathroom, or it could pay for a getaway with your family.

The concept of a savings account is aligned to Joseph's counsel when he was called upon to interpret Pharaoh's dream. This was Joseph's counsel after he had finished interpreting the dream:

> *Let Pharaoh do this, and let him appoint officers over the land, to collect one-fifth of the produce of the land of Egypt in the seven plentiful years. And let them gather all the food of those good years that are coming, and store up grain under the authority of Pharaoh, and let them keep food in the cities. Then that food shall be as a reserve for the land for the seven years of famine which shall be in the land of Egypt, that the land may not perish during the famine. (Genesis 41:34–36 NKJV).*

They invest regularly

Financially mature people look for quality information about money to try and understand how investments work.

I'd say that the best source of quality information about money and investing can be found in the Bible. You can also obtain some from your financial planner at your local bank. There are many good financial planning seminars, many of which may be available online or in person near where you live. Once they become comfortable with their understanding, they can proceed to invest.

For a Christian, one of the great investment vehicles is tithing and general giving. Financially mature Christians understand the concept of tithing primarily as a demonstration of their **love** for God and their **obedience** to his command about tithing. But according to prophet Malachi, tithing is also an investment vehicle. For some religious and self-righteous individuals, saying that tithing is a form of investment would be considered sacrilegious. But here's what that famous scripture says, "Bring all the tithes into the storehouse, That there may be food in My house, And try Me now in this," Says the Lord of hosts, "*If I will not open for you the windows of heaven And pour out for you such blessing That there will not be room enough to receive it.*" (Malachi 3:10 NKJV). (Italics have been added to indicate discussion points below.)

> *For some religious, self-righteous individuals, saying that tithing is a form of investment will be considered sacrilegious.*

We can clearly see in the italicized words how God is promising a "return" on our tithe. The return is to pour out a blessing that will be so huge that we will end up with a crisis of containment. But that'll be a good kind of crisis to face, won't it? Therefore, when you tithe you shouldn't think that you're throwing away your money. No, it's actually an investment. Anyone who tithes faithfully will agree that God is also faithful in keeping his promise of "pouring out a blessing."

KEY TAKE AWAY

- A carefully laid foundation is important for a marriage that's going to flourish over the long haul.
- Marriage readiness can be measured in terms of physical, spiritual, emotional, and financial maturity.
- Self-awareness is essential in sustaining long-term relationships, especially a healthy marriage.
- Husbands must pursue maturity more aggressively so that they can lead their families more effectively.
- A mature person has habits, traits, and behaviours that others can look up to.
- Good financial management skills are required to achieve financial stability, which will eliminate the tension that financial issues often bring to marriages.
- Tithing is a show of love for God and obedience to his command. But tithing is also an investment vehicle with a guaranteed amazing return.

CHAPTER THREE

HOW TO START A RELATIONSHIP

Several important questions occupy a huge real estate in the minds of most singles, particularly those who are in their teens or early twenties. Some examples of these questions are:

- How do I start a relationship now that I am coming of age?
- What is the ideal place for me to meet that cute guy?
- Where do I go to find that beautiful girl?
- What is the right approach once I come across a girl that I like?

These are all legitimate questions. It's the focus of this chapter to provide some general information that'll help singles who are grappling with these types of questions. I call the information general because there's no hard and fast rule about where and how to meet that cute guy or that beautiful girl.

The Most Important First Step

For a Christian, the most important first step that should never be skipped in starting a relationship is spiritual preparation. As I've said earlier, for a Christian, marriage is a spiritual undertaking. Consequently, spiritual preparation forms a key part of laying the foundation. If you get it right within this first step, you will have begun on a very good note. How you start with this most important step sets the tone for how you'll conduct yourself during the dating period. And ultimately, it'll also help you throughout the duration of your marriage.

You can be spiritually prepared by making sure that you're certain about your salvation, as well, you're in an intimate relationship with God. You have unequivocally accepted that your spiritual life is important to you, and your spiritual life forms the basis for all your decisions, choices, and actions. In fact, you have come to appreciate the value of your relationship with God to the point that you are unwilling to trade it for anything. Jesus taught that we should seek first and foremost the kingdom of God and his righteousness, and every other thing shall be ours (Matthew 6:33).

I'll reiterate again that it's going to serve you well if you can grow to the point where you know that the Bible is the highest authority in all matters of the Christian faith, and it's the most reliable reference manual necessary for victorious living. This level of conviction is important because it'll sustain you through all phases of life.

> *In fact, you have come to appreciate the value of your relationship with God to the point that you will be unwilling to trade it for anything.*

The second essential part of your life you'll need to hone is your prayer life. You understand prayer as a dialogue between you and God. You're learning to talk to God and how to hear him speak back to you. As you talk to God about your desire for a relationship, you need to be able to hear when he speaks to you about it. For example, God may lead you to be at a place where you will meet that special someone you have been praying about.

Let us see the prayer of Abraham's servant who went to find a wife for Isaac among Abraham's kindred as an example. This is how he prayed:

> *Then he said, "O Lord God of my master Abraham, please give me success this day, and show kindness to my master Abraham. Behold, here I stand by the well of water, and the sons of the men of the city are coming out to draw water. Now let it be that the young woman to whom I say, 'Please let down your pitcher that I may drink,' and she says, 'Drink, and I will also give your camels a drink'—let her be the one You have appointed for Your servant Isaac. And by this I will know that You have shown kindness to my master. And it happened, before he had finished speaking, that behold, Rebekah, who was born to Bethuel, son of Milcah, the wife of Nahor, Abraham's brother, came out with her pitcher on her shoulder. Now the young woman was very beautiful to behold, a virgin; no man had known her. And she went down to the well, filled her pitcher, and came up. And the servant ran to meet her and said, 'Please let me drink a little water from your pitcher.' So she said, 'Drink, my lord.' Then she quickly let her pitcher down*

to her hand, and gave him a drink. And when she had finished giving him a drink, she said, 'I will draw water for your camels also, until they have finished drinking.' Then she quickly emptied her pitcher into the trough, ran back to the well to draw water, and drew for all his camels. And the man, wondering at her, remained silent so as to know whether the Lord had made his journey prosperous or not." (Genesis 24:12–21 NKJV)

This is a good sample prayer that someone who is believing God will provide for an opportunity to meet a life partner can pray. The exciting part is how God answered this prayer. The verses show how faithful God is in answering a prayer that is prayed in faith.

Often, it comes as a shock for singles to discover that they're finding it difficult or are confused about who is the right person for them. Meanwhile, they're always in the midst of many other singles. This probably explains why it isn't uncommon to see singles dash in and out of relationships. A simple prayer of faith made in the belief that God answers prayer is the key. That is, you must develop a childlike faith in your prayer life and trust God to answer your prayer. You must also possess some ability to hear and discern God's leading or speaking. That ability can save you from a frustrating experience of going into relationships that end even before they start.

In addition, I've heard many singles—both young and mature adults—confess that they can't find someone to marry. In fact, some single women out of frustration have said that it's nearly impossible to find a man with the qualities of a good husband. They say that men who possess qualities of a good husband have all been taken. My advice to them is simple: don't become despondent about not being found by that great guy yet, because there are still many solid men out there with great qualities that any woman would desire in a man.

> *Don't become despondent about not being found by that great guy yet, as there are still many solid men out there with great qualities any woman would desire in a man.*

What Is the Ideal Place to Meet a Life Partner

This is another question most singles commonly ask, and it's an important question to ask. The fact that many young people need help with how to meet that special someone is evident in the kind of ideas many of them have about the issue. When asked what they have done so far to meet someone, some say that they started frequenting gyms, bars, and nightclubs with the hope they might meet that special someone.

Therefore, to answer this question, let me suggest that certain places may not be the best place to search for a long-term relationship. For example, bars, pubs, and nightclubs may not be the best place to meet a fellow Christian with whom to start a relationship. Some people would argue that not everyone who attends bars and pubs is a heavy drinker. However, I'll argue that the chances you'll meet a Christian single you'd be proud of in a bar or pub are not high.

> *I will argue that the chances you will meet a Christian single that you would be proud of in a bar or pub are not high.*

As a rule of thumb, you want to meet your future spouse in a place that you'd be proud to talk about throughout your married life. "How did you meet" is one question that you are likely to answer frequently as a married person, especially in the early days of your marriage. Of course, I am aware that there are decent people who on occasion go for a drink with friends, to celebrate a birthday, or some other important life event. Usually, such occasions are few and far in between, which I believe is safe for a Christian.

> *Marriage is the most important relationship decision that I'll ever make, so why should I go into it with some doubts in my mind?*

First and foremost, there is a need to rely heavily on God, who is the author of creativity to arrange that special encounter with your future life partner. That's the ultimate way to start a relationship as a Christian. Here are more examples of possible places to meet your future life partner:

- A church service.
- A young adults' fellowship.
- A Christian single's event.
- A social gathering, where the attendees are likely to be Christian singles.

- A wedding.
- An occasion where a trusted friend introduces you to someone.
- A vacation.
- A high school (for teenagers and young adults).
- A college campus.
- At work.
- At a shopping mall.
- At a restaurant.
- On a public transit bus or train.
- In a park.
- At a professional networking event.

You need to simply trust God to be faithful to arrange that special encounter, which you both can talk and laugh about decades after your wedding.

Online Dating

Online dating sites have dramatically increased in popularity since the dawn of the twenty-first century, and some sites have been specifically created for Christian singles. I'm ignorant about their mode of operation, and I am unsure what screening mechanisms the operators have put in place to shut out unscrupulous individuals from joining. One should be aware that some may join these sites with the sole purpose of taking advantage of those who are genuinely looking for a relationship.

For that reason, while I won't discourage believers from considering online dating sites, I will caution that they should be careful and do their due diligence before getting involved. It's common knowledge that many of such sites have become avenues where dubious people go to rob genuine, unsuspecting relationship seekers of their life savings.

> *While I will not discourage believers from considering online dating sites, I will caution that they should be careful and do their due diligence before getting involved.*

One important counsel that I'll give regarding your desire to meet your future spouse is to never be anxious about it. Be calm and fully assured that God is faithful, and he makes all things beautiful in its time (Ecclesiastes 3:11). It is not advisable to try to go ahead of God in your quest to get anything. Apostle Paul wrote to the Philippians that they should "Be anxious for nothing, but in everything by prayer and supplication, with thanksgiving, let your requests be made known to God; and the peace of God, which surpasses all understanding, will guard your hearts and minds through Christ Jesus." (Philippians 4:6–7 NKJV).

You should be patient as you trust God to lead you to your future life partner. If you aren't careful, a thought will creep into your heart from a strange source that you should hurry and do whatever it takes to meet him or her. If you don't resist that temptation, you'll go ahead and hurriedly do whatever it takes, and in the process your judgment will be clouded beyond your ability to discern what God may be saying about the situation.

James 1:2–4 says, "My brethren, count it all joy when you fall into various trials, knowing that the testing of your faith produces patience. But let patience have its perfect work, that you may be perfect and complete, lacking nothing."

I've referenced this passage to encourage singles who may be getting weary of waiting. For such singles, it'd be right to say that their faith is being tested. This passage admonishes that you should be careful to know that the testing of your faith produces patience. And when allowed, patience can have its perfect work, which will then lead to your wholeness. Without question, wholeness is a great place to be as a Christian.

Both *anxiety* and *impatience* have proven to lead people into making poor or second-rate choices. That's why I strongly recommend that you work as hard as you can to control anxiety and impatience as you are on the lookout to start a long-term relationship.

> *Impatience has proven to lead people into making poor or second-rate choices.*

How to Stay Calm While Waiting to Start a Relationship

It isn't easy to wait for anything, particularly something that is important to you. Our fast-paced life, which characterizes our digital age, has increased our inability to patiently wait for anything. However, one's ability to patiently wait is a priceless attribute. Prophet Isaiah has this to say about waiting, "But those who wait on the Lord shall renew their strength; they shall mount up with wings as eagles; they shall run, and not be weary, they shall walk, and not faint." (Isaiah 40:31 NKJV). Waiting patiently on the Lord is a guaranteed way of renewing our strength. We can see how he likens such strength to that of the eagle, the most powerful bird. Waiting also sustains and equips us for patient perseverance.

In Philippians the Apostle Paul admonishes that we shouldn't be anxious, but by prayer and supplication, with thanksgiving, to let our requests be made known to God; and the peace of God, which surpasses all understanding, will guard our hearts and minds through Christ Jesus. In this verse we learn how peace comes when we eschew anxiety. And the antidote to anxiety is to learn to be prayerful with a grateful heart. I've provided four proven suggestions below with some examples of how you can use them to arrive at a place of rest and tranquility as you wait for that beautiful encounter with your future partner.

Never forget the past faithfulness of God

It's important to keep in view the past faithfulness and goodness of God. Never forget the track record of his loving kindness. I believe every child of God must have repeatedly experienced the faithfulness as well as the loving kindness of God in their lives. I find this to be one of the most important tools available to a believer in creating a sense of calmness even during delays or storms of life. To use this tool successfully, it would help to develop a habit of recounting the faithfulness of God to you with a thankful heart. God told the children of Israel:

> *and when your herds and your flocks multiply, and your silver and your gold are multiplied, and all that you have is multiplied; when your heart is lifted up, and you forget the Lord your God who brought you out of the land of Egypt, from the house of bondage; who led you through that great and terrible wilderness, in which were fiery serpents and scorpions and thirsty land where there was no water; who brought water for you out of the flinty rock; who fed you in the wilderness with manna, which your fathers did not know, that He might humble you and that He might test you, to do you good in the end—then you say in your heart, 'My power and the might of my hand have gained me this wealth.'* ***And you shall remember the Lord your God, for it is He who gives you power to get wealth,*** *that He may establish His covenant which He swore to your fathers, as it is this day. (Deuteronomy 8:13-18 NKJV)*

We can see from these verses how Moses reiterated the goodness of God and his miraculous deliverances of the children of Israel. He went further to recount how the Lord cared and provided for them in very special circumstances. He then demanded of them, "and you shall remember the Lord your God." Remembering the Lord's faithfulness is very beneficial because it communicates several important messages. First, when you remember the Lord's faithfulness and goodness, you are effectively saying that you are grateful for what he has done for you in the past. In other words, remembering his faithfulness is effectively saying that he is bigger and beyond any situation we're facing including your desire to get married.

Second, being thankful to God for his faithfulness means that you know him from his precedence. You are saying that based on God's faithfulness in that past, you know that he is more than able to meet your present need of finding a partner. You are acknowledging that he has done a lot for you in the past, and he will continue to give you the desires of your heart. As can be seen from several biblical accounts, we know that King David was a uniquely good individual, but thankfulness was arguably one of his many great attributes that earned him the description of being "a man after God's heart."

Thirdly, I also find recounting God's faithfulness to be a powerful and effective means of building your faith. As you begin to recount God's faithfulness and blessings in your life, simultaneously your faith will start to rise. The anxiety that comes along with the doubt of finding a relationship will melt away, while the confidence that it won't be long before your partner walks into your waiting arms will steadily grow to an impressive level. This is precisely what happened during David's encounter with Goliath.

> *"But David said to Saul, "Your servant used to keep his father's sheep, and when a lion or a bear came and took a lamb out of the flock, I went out after it and struck it, and delivered the lamb from its mouth; and when it arose against me, I caught it by its beard, and struck and killed it. Your servant has killed both lion and bear; and this uncircumcised Philistine will be like one of them, seeing*

he has defied the armies of the living God." ***Moreover, David said, "The Lord, who delivered me from the paw of the lion and from the paw of the bear, He will deliver me from the hand of this Philistine."***
(1 Samuel 17:34-37 NKJV)(Emphasis for discussion)

Pay close attention to how David recounted his past victories and then concluded with a powerful statement that instantly turned him into an unstoppable conqueror. This is a paraphrase of what he said: The Lord who has previously given me victory over the lion and the bear is still very much alive and he will give me victory over this uncircumcised Philistine as well. David pleasantly remembered what great feats they were to wrestle and overpower the lion and the bear. He never forgot that God was responsible for those special victories. Notice also that David's words were not merely words, but I see his words as prayers. These words invoked the powers of heaven to earn him victory over Goliath.

Therefore, as you wait to meet your life partner, learn to be thoughtful in acknowledging with confidence God's past faithfulness and goodness to you. If you have a short memory that you cannot remember God's past goodness, then I suggest that you keep a journal where you write down each time he intervenes on your behalf or as you remember them. You'll be pleasantly shocked at the goodness of God.

Here is a sample prayer that you can pray:

Father, I thank you for your loving kindness over my life. I thank you for every provision that you have made available to me. I thank you for my health, my job, my home, my friends, and all that I have. I am grateful that you have given me everything that pertains to life and godliness. I acknowledge you as the source of everything that I have. Above all, I thank you for the gift of your Son Jesus, who is my Lord and Saviour. Your faithfulness and goodness are beyond description.

Now, I have come of age—both physically and spiritually—and I am ready to get married and settle down. My eyes are on you to arrange for me to meet with my life partner, wherever she or he may be on the face of the earth, because I know that nothing is too difficult for you. I also know that you make everything beautiful in its time. You have done so much for me in the past, and I know that you are more than able to put me in touch with my future partner. Therefore, I am not going to fret. I will remain calm and wait for your perfect timing. You are never too early nor too late. You are always right on time. I thank you in advance for answering my prayer because I have prayed in Jesus' Name, AMEN.

You can tweak this template to suit your specific circumstances, while carefully noting that a thankful heart is a healthy heart that knows how to move the hand of God to work on its behalf.

Know that with God, delay is never a denial

Ruthanne was a high-flying investment banker working for one of her country's leading commercial banks. She came from a strong evangelical Christian family background. Throughout her high school and university days, her life was what would be fittingly described as triangular. That is, home—school and reading—church. She was an honours student who graduated at the top of her class.

Ruthanne joined the workforce upon graduation where she continued with her excellent work ethic. Due to her performance, coupled with God's favour, she started enjoying accelerated promotions. As the saying goes when you're busy you lose track of time. This was so true of Ruthanne, and as her thirty-second birthday was just a week away she decided to take time to deeply reflect on her busy life. It was during this reflection that she realized she'd already been working for ten years since graduating from university.

Although, Ruthanne had occasionally thought about marriage before, in the days leading up to her thirty-second birthday she thought about it more seriously. Her birthday came and went with a fresh consciousness that she was now thirty-two years old and marriage became a key priority for her. As a result, Ruthanne determined in her heart that she was going to start praying much more regularly about a relationship. She had been praying for a year about meeting someone, even as her next birthday was approaching. According to her, she was increasingly becoming conscious of just how fast time was moving. She could hardly believe that she was almost thirty-three years old.

On her thirty-sixth birthday, Ruthanne's siblings and parents organized a nice dinner for her. According to her, when she got home from her birthday dinner, she went straight to bed with her party clothes on sobbing uncontrollably. She cried her heart out that night. In the middle of the night, she reached out for her journal and with a heavy heart, penned this emotional and agonizing prayer:

> *Heavenly Father, you are all-knowing. So you know how I have served you from my childhood. My parents home-schooled me. I have been a good girl all my life. Now, tell me Lord, what is happening to me that at thirty-six, a good Christian girl is not yet married, I've not even started a relationship. Father, I'm upset, very upset about the whole thing. Have I been wasting my time all these years keeping myself chaste so that I'll remain a vessel of honor to you? Doesn't it pay to serve you anymore? Most of my acquaintances who don't even know or serve you are well settled with families of their own. What's happening? Why have you forsaken me? What have I done wrong, Lord?*

Ruthanne kept sobbing as she poured out her heart to the Lord on her thirty-sixth birthday. She lamented before the Lord that night until she had no more strength left in her. She got so tired that she didn't even know when she drifted off to sleep. She slept until the early hours of the next day. Ruthanne narrated how she had a sweet dream or perhaps a vision. She wasn't sure. In that dream, she was in a church service and the pastor was teaching on the life of Hannah, how she was childless several years after she had been married.

The pastor took his text from 1 Samuel 1:1-17. He taught verse by verse from that passage. Then he came to verse ten, which says this: "And she was in bitterness of soul, and prayed to the Lord and wept in anguish." That's how bitter I have been about my situation, Ruthanne recalled as she listened very attentively to the message.

Then the pastor continued his teaching until he got to verse seventeen where prophet Eli prayed for Hannah and said, "Go in peace, and the God of Israel grant your petition which you have asked of Him."

As the pastor continued with his teaching, he got to verse nineteen and twenty. Those verses read thus: "Then they rose early in the morning and worshiped before the Lord, and returned and came to their house at Ramah. *And Elkanah knew Hannah his wife, and the Lord remembered her.* So it came to pass in the process of time that *Hannah conceived and bore a son*, and called his name Samuel, saying, 'Because I have asked for him from the Lord.'" (Italics for discussion)

And the pastor continued his verse by verse teaching before he jumped to 1 Samuel 2:21: "And the Lord visited Hannah, so that she conceived and bore three sons and two daughters. Meanwhile, the child Samuel grew before the Lord."

The pastor took the time to explain the faithfulness of God shown to Hannah by remembering Hannah prayers, and God answered her prayer as he gave her Samuel. But he didn't stop there. After Hannah sacrificially gave her only son to the service of the Lord, God compensated her with three more sons and two daughters. The woman who was written off as barren became a mother of six children. That's the faithfulness of God, the pastor stressed. As the high point of his message, he continued by stating that there's somebody in this service who has been expecting a miracle from the Lord for many years. That person is a single lady. I have a message for that person from the Lord, "Delay is not denial!" The Lord has remembered you, weep no more. The Lord has heard your prayer. He has turned your mourning into dancing. Start thanking God for your miracle. Your miracle is now yours!

The Lord has remembered you, weep no more.

Suddenly, Ruth woke up, and behold it was a long and sweet dream. Although it was only a dream, she found so much comfort from it. For several days following her dream, she spent time studying and meditating on the first two chapters of the book of 1 Samuel. She strongly believed that it was the Lord that had visited her in that dream. The pastor's concluding words kept ringing in her mind—Delay is not denial. The Lord has remembered you, weep no more. The Lord has heard your prayer. He has turned your mourning into dancing. Start thanking God for your miracle. Your miracle is now yours! She believed that those words were meant for her and she received them into her spirit. She kept repeating them to herself for several weeks.

About two months after her dream, a gentleman named Jim came to set up an investment account at Ruthanne's bank. By divine arrangement, the amount of money Jim was going to invest was so significant that only Ruthanne was high up enough to manage. As Jim was leaving Ruthanne's office, they were sure to exchange their business cards. That same evening, Jim called and thanked Ruthanne for her help and professionalism earlier that day. Ruthanne appreciated Jim's call but quickly added that she was just doing her job. Jim went further to ask if she was available for dinner the following evening. Ruthanne quickly checked through her calendar and confirmed that indeed, her evening was open. Jim called a high-end Italian restaurant and booked a reservation for dinner for two.

They both enjoyed the evening out together. Jim called her the next day and thanked her for spending the time with him the previous evening. A week later, Jim offered Ruthanne another invitation for dinner. Again, Ruthanne confirmed her availability. During this second dinner, they discussed more personal things such as faith, age, and family background. They were both pleasantly shocked at the striking similarities in their backgrounds. In fact, Jim was also home-schooled, and his parents were leading members of their local church. Jim was only one year older than Ruthanne.

The relationship between Ruthanne and Jim developed quickly, yet intentionally. Jim proposed six months after their first date, and they married three months later. The duo is now enjoying a happy married life with two beautiful children running around the house and keeping them both busy.

As I talk to other singles, I find that many have a story similar to that of Ruthanne. But let me encourage you that in fact, your similarities will not only be in the wait and the tears, but your praise report can also be like hers. Perhaps, like most young ladies, you wanted to get married by the age of twenty-six, but now you find yourself in the mid thirties or even older and you have lots of questions to ask God. Of course, I may not fully understand your own unique circumstances. But I know one thing: with God, delay doesn't mean denial. Yes, you may be enduring a delay, but God hasn't denied you your desire for a life partner. Keep your eyes on him. Your praise report is going to come sooner than you may realize.

> *I know one thing: with God, delay doesn't mean denial.*

Keep learning about dating and what makes a marriage great

There are so many exciting and eye-popping things to be learned about the institution of marriage, including how singles need to conduct themselves during courtship. About what it takes to lead a successful and fun-filled marriage. Unfortunately, not every single understands that they'll be in a position of strength if they take the time to prepare before going into a dating relationship, as well as preparing themselves for marriage itself. I highly recommend that no single person should sit by and wait until they start a relationship before they start groping around in the dark to discover how to be purposeful in their courtship to make it the most productive and worthwhile. Be proactive and get ahead of the curve.

I am not aware of many books that focus mainly on courtship; hence, the Holy Spirit has inspired me to write this one. If your local church has a program for singles or an intending couples' class, take advantage of it and learn as much as you can. In fact, if there is no such arrangement in place at your local church, find a couple whose family life you admire and approach them to be able to pick their brains on the subject of marriage. Furthermore, you might ask your pastor or his wife if there is any plan to start a single's or intending couples' class soon. You can also ask around if there are any good singles or intending couples' classes available in your city or town that you could enrol in. Pursue knowledge about marriage as if your life depends on it because it actually does.

Perhaps, somebody may ask you, "Why go that far when you haven't even started a relationship yet?" Well, here are my four answers to that question; first, it's a demonstration of faith and confidence that you'll soon start a relationship, and that you want to be ready even before the relationship actually begins. Second, remember, the book of Hebrews says that faith is the substance of things hoped for, the evidence of things not seen (Hebrews 11:1 NKJV). Preparing for how you'll handle your dating experience goes to show that you are very certain that you're going to start a relationship sooner than later. The third reason is that when the relationship does start, you may likely be too euphoric about it to actually learn about dating. And the fourth reason is that, ultimately, it's a remedy against idling and bemoaning your situation, that it's taking so long for you to start a relationship. Therefore, get busy by preparing for your relationship and God will bring the person to you.

Make sure you're not competing with anyone.

Starting a relationship is usually one of the highest priorities for most singles, particularly teenagers and young adults. I'm sure those high school days will quickly come to mind when you talk about dating. As one sees their friends and peers pairing up into relationships, one begins to feel that they're missing out. Although, most of those high school dates don't normally develop into a long-term relationship, they're the starting point where healthy attitudes about relationships may be learned.

The most important point to understand and keep very close to your heart is to assure yourself that everyone's path is different. Your path in life as an individual is totally different from everyone else's, including your best friends and even your siblings. Such understanding will greatly help you to be at peace with yourself that it doesn't really matter if your peers and friends are in relationships ahead of you. You'd never be motivated to desperately go into a relationship and get married simply because those around you are getting married. There's an ancient saying about life that states "It's not how far, but how well." Your real focus should be on aligning yourself with God's timing to make sure that you get it right the first time.

> *Your path of life as an individual is totally different from everyone else's, including your best friends and even your siblings.*

Although her story is that of barrenness and not about dating relationships, Sarah's unique story should be a good lesson for all times and for every believer. As we all know, Sarah was barren and had lost confidence that she would ever have a child. Hence, she erroneously decided in her wisdom to go ahead of God and gave her handmaid to Abraham to become his second wife. That Bible account says:

> *Now Sarai, Abram's wife, had borne him no children. And she had an Egyptian maidservant whose name was Hagar. So Sarai said to Abram, 'See now, the Lord has restrained me from bearing children. Please, go in to my maid; perhaps I shall obtain children by her.' And Abram heeded the voice of Sarai. Then Sarai, Abram's wife, took Hagar her maid, the Egyptian, and gave her to her husband Abram to be his wife, after Abram had dwelt ten years in the land of Canaan (Genesis 16:1-3 NKJV).*

Sadly, once Hagar became pregnant, she turned and started looking down on Sarah (Genesis 16:4-5). But the good news is that God wasn't done with Sarah yet as eventually, God caused her to conceive and have Isaac (Genesis 21:12 NKJV).

And Isaac had Jacob, and out of Jacob came the twelve tribes of Israel. And out of Judah, one of the twelve tribes came Jesus Christ who is our Lord and Saviour. Hagar made it look as if she and Sarah were in a competition. But God kept his promise to Abraham and what a great multitude is the number of those who are Sarah's extended offspring today. Whatever you may be waiting for, be it a life partner or any other thing, you should never be tempted to go about it as if you're in a competition with anyone. In case someone tries to pick on you and tempt you to act as though you're in a competition, remember what Ecclesiastes says, "The end of a thing is better than its beginning; The patient in spirit is better than the proud in spirit." (Ecclesiastes 7:8 NKJV).

Be certain to assure yourself that God is not done with you just yet. When he's done with you, your end will be more glorious than the current situation in which people are seeing you.

> *Whatever you may be waiting for, be it a life partner or any other thing, you should never to tempted to go about it as if you're in a competition with anyone.*

KEY TAKE AWAY

- The key starting point in your search for a life partner is to ensure you have an intimate relationship with God.
- An intimate relationship with God can be achieved through the quality of your prayer life and the extent that you believe in God's Word.
- An effective prayer is the prayer that is said with childlike faith.
- You can meet your future spouse just about anywhere.
- It is not recommended that you go to bars, pubs, or nightclubs in search of your future life partner.
- If you want to explore online dating sites, be vigilant because cyberspace is known to be a convenient hiding place for unscrupulous people.
- As you trust God to lead you to your future spouse, rid yourself of anxiety and impatience.
- Keys to help you remain calm as you wait to start a relationship include:
    - Keep the faithfulness of God in view.

- Know that with God, delay is never a denial.
- Keep learning about dating etiquette and married life.
- Assure yourself that you're not in a competition with anyone.

CHAPTER FOUR

LEVERAGE THE COURTSHIP PERIOD

Courtship is a period of mutual discovery. This is the ideal time to get to know the person you're dating very well. The couple should take full advantage of this important period to study and thoroughly understand each other. I'll urge the reader to take particular note of the word "study"! The overarching goal of courtship is that at the end, the couple will be able to confidently answer the crucial question of *"are we a good fit for each other or not"*. It's important that both individuals can confidently answer this question without a hint of doubt in their mind.

It's advisable that should any doubt exist in the mind of either individual then they should be courageous enough to refrain from going ahead with their marriage plans until they're sure that their doubts are resolved. To help the couple make this decision, here's a suggested rational thought process for the two people involved: Marriage is the most important relationship decision that I'll ever make, so why should I go into it with some doubts in my mind?

To make an effective use of the courtship period, both individuals should make every effort to resist the temptation of becoming emotionally trapped, or trapped because your sense of judgment has been compromised. We all have heard of the adage that "love is blind." If you get emotionally trapped, you could be blind to the otherwise apparent indicators that he or she may not be the right person to be your lifetime partner.

I have had the opportunity of listening to many divorced individuals who have confessed that, with the benefit of hindsight they saw some of the "red flags" that came to be responsible for the failure of their marriage. Almost all of them that I have talked to confessed that they ignored all those "red flags" during the courtship period. Many of the things that negatively affect a marriage don't suddenly show up. They're often there from the beginning of the relationship, but people just miss them because they were emotionally trapped.

One lady whose marriage did not work out told me that she and her husband fought on their first night together following their wedding. What a horribly unfortunate way to start a marriage. This was her second marriage, and although this woman was in her sixties with grandchildren, she still got it wrong.

Many others have confessed that they had dated for so long, and everyone important to them knew about the relationship. As such, they simply didn't know how to breakup the relationship after being a couple for such a long time.

Some have reasoned that it would look bad on them, because people would know that they were the ones that opted out of the relationship. Many said this because they didn't know that it isn't wrong to end a dating relationship if they have a justifiable reason to do so. Regardless of whose fault it is, it won't reflect badly on you if you end the relationship for the right reasons.

Others, especially ladies, have confessed to being scared to end things after considering how long it took them to start this relationship. If their current relationship was unsuccessful, they weren't sure that they would be able to find another man. The question for such ladies to answer is this: Why do you live a life believing God will give you the desires of your heart, but doubt his ability and faithfulness to give you an ideal life partner as he has promised in his word? (Psalms 37:4).

Going ahead with a relationship that has clear "red flags" negates the purpose of courtship, which is the period to determine if you are suited for each other or not. You must decide between these two options:

- Breakup a courtship that has observable pitfalls.
- Ignore the pitfalls and proceed, but with the near certainty that the marriage will be doomed to fail even before it starts.

> *Why do you live a life believing God will give you your heart's desires but doubt His ability and faithfulness to give you an ideal life partner as He has promised in His Word?*

Potential Areas to Find Differences

Many couples whose marriages have failed often cite a lack of compatibility as the reason for divorce. Unfortunately, as I stated above, most of the differences were there the whole time. In this section of the book, I will help you understand some of the areas where differences are most likely to come.

Note that you can celebrate the areas where there is compatibility between the two of you, but it's likely that there will be some incompatibilities too. Pay close attention to those areas where incompatibilities exist as they'll provide some clues about potential areas of marital conflict.

Personality

It is not abnormal to find that there are personality differences between the two of you. In fact, personality differences should be expected. There are many factors that will account for these differences, some of which include family background, environment, culture, education, profession, and so on.

Here are some questions to guide you in unearthing personality differences between you and your partner:

What is your level of self-awareness?

Do you both know your personalities well enough? Self-awareness leads to good self-management which in turn helps to manage your relationships better. For example, if you're a perfectionist, which is a negative trait and your partner is not, you'll need to be careful not to place an undue demand on your spouse to do things in your own perfectionist way.

What is his or her temperament?

If one of you has a hot temper, you'll need to take steps to learn how to take control of your anger. One of the key steps may be to take a Bible study course about anger management. Some people in that situation have used professional services of psychotherapists to learn how to manage their anger.

Is there flexibility with choices and decision-making?

For some people, it is either their way or no way. Once they make up their mind about a situation, they leave no room for any negotiation and you must either take it or leave it. As life is about making choices and decisions, carefully consider how your family life will be like with such a spouse who'll always insists on having their own way.

Are they an extrovert or an introvert?

Each of these personality types has their own strengths and weaknesses. As part of your courtship, try and understand how best to manage with each other's personality. Carefully consider if each partner will be a good complement for their extroverted or introverted personality. Experience has shown that sometimes, two extroverts may find it difficult to work well together.

Does one person have an exaggerated opinion of themselves, or do both individuals have a healthy sense of personal self-worth?

A person with an exaggerated opinion of themselves are often proud. James 4:6 says that God resists the proud, but he gives grace to the humble. Humility is a virtue, pride is not! Would it be a problem for you to marry somebody whom God is resisting?

What are each other's strengths and weaknesses

Getting to know what the strengths and weaknesses are of someone you're dating is important for several reasons. It'll help you to know what to expect them to do well or not to do as well. Based on your knowledge of each other's strengths and weaknesses you'll know in advance how best you'll complement each other. For example, there's always an expectation that as a pastor's wife one will be confident standing in front of people and expressing herself. Recently, during our annual conference I privately asked our guest speaker if his wife would be gracious enough to greet the conference attendees. With the knowledge of his wife's weaknesses, he asked me to excuse his wife from standing up to say even few words during the conference.

Do they possess good social skills?

It's good to know your partner's comfort level when in a social setting. This also is linked to knowing how outgoing or not they may be.

Do they know how to and are willing to cook?

Both the husband and the wife should be able cook, although this task typically falls more on the lady's side of expectations. There's also a cultural dimension to this issue. In majority of cultures, most ladies don't mind owning this responsibility. Yet in other cultures, an increasing number of young females are beginning to question why they should take on that responsibility in the home. Which culture your would-be partner falls into is important to know ahead of getting married. That way, the culture expectation and the responsibility will be managed much better.

Are they a neat and tidy person, or are they the one who leave things all over the house?

On the surface, some may consider this issue trivial. But for many it's a serious irritant. It won't be too long before you'll know this aspect of yourselves. This can easily be known as you begin to spend considerable amount of time in each other's homes.

Do they love the Lord, or are they one who goes to church twice a year—on Easter Sunday and on Christmas Day?

You can find out about their spiritual background through the books that they read. Where do they worship? Do they know the name of the pastor? How involved are they in church? Do they belong to any group in the church? Who are their friends? Amos 3:3 says that two cannot work together unless they are in agreement. The adage that states "Show me your friend, and I will tell you who you are" is also true most of the time.

Always keep in mind that the overarching goal of these sample questions is to get to know this person who may one day become "one flesh" with you. It's not about being a perfectionist, or a fault detective who insists on someone who's flawless, because such a person doesn't exist anywhere on the face of the earth. If you're intentional with your dating, it won't be too long and neither will it require a lot of effort to figure all the answers to the above questions.

These questions will help you to take a step back and ask yourself if, with the knowledge of who you're, you are going to be a good complement for them or not. What areas of their life will you support to strengthen? Or what areas of your life will you need their help to become more complete? It is a bidirectional consideration. The Bible says that iron sharpens iron. (Proverbs 27:17).

This rule of thumb cannot be stated too many times: You should be concerned if you have a serious relationship with someone who isn't a Christian. Or with someone who hasn't mastered what Apostle Paul referred to as "the first principles of the oracles of God." It isn't good if you must be your spouse's babysitter because you're likely not going to do a good job of that. Even if somebody else is helping you babysit them, you'll be dragged down at home, one way or the other.

An example of this issue was a young couple, named Kirsten and Kerr. I knew them after they were already married with three young kids. I can confirm that Kirsten clearly came across as someone who loved the Lord and was spiritually mature. Kerr, not so much. They were struggling in their marriage. Kirsten really wanted Kerr to mature spiritually so he could lead her and their children. As someone who desperately needed help, she opened up to me about their struggles. At the core of their problem was Kerr's pervasive addiction to pornography, which was rapidly destroying their marriage. Once, he was caught watching porn at work and he received his final warning. He had received psychotherapy counselling many times in the past, but obviously he needed much more than the psychologists could offer him.

At the core of their problem was Kerr's pervasive addiction to pornography, which was rapidly destroying their marriage.

I asked Kirsten how their relationship had started and grew into marriage. Being eager about getting help, she confided in me, "I knew the Lord before I met Kerr, unfortunately, I didn't pay attention to where he stood from a spiritual standpoint. However, I was optimistic that his becoming a committed Christian would not be a problem." She admitted with despair, "now, I know where I got it wrong." Then she asked with her eyes welling up with tears, "please, can you help in mentoring him so he can take his place as a responsible husband, father, and spiritual head of the family?"

I assured Kirsten of my willingness to help, but knowing what she was up against I was careful not to over promise. I knew that Kerr's addiction to pornography was at the root of their struggles. Kerr and I met once for coffee to try and build rapport. Suddenly, he stopped coming to church altogether. Before I could find out what was happening, he had moved out their home to live on his own. Eventually, he filed for divorce, and he left Kirsten with three children to raise on her own.

I am sad to add this part of the story. But I had to add it to make sure their lesson is learned by other singles. Most probably due to the burden of what happened to her marriage with Kerr, Kirsten later got married to someone else who was not a Christian and her personal walk with the Lord is now in serious doubt. But I believe it all started with the failure of her first marriage.

Therefore, let me reiterate once again that differences are not a bad thing. Differences may help you to complement each other. If you aren't overly emotional and blind about the relationship, differences will help you to decide if you'll be a good fit for each other over the long-term or not. Based on that understanding, you'll be able to make an informed decision on whether the relationship should continue into marriage or not.

> *If you are not overly emotional and blind about the relationship, differences will help you decide if you will be a good fit for each other over the long-term or not.*

Family backgrounds

Again, let me state that differences that come from family backgrounds are normal. It must be acknowledged that no two families will ever be the same. It's also true that how and where you're raised will certainly influence how you approach things, your outlook on life, your choices, and your value system. Therefore, you should expect differences in this area.

Here's a sample list of questions to guide you:

- Do they come from a Christian family?
- Are you both well aligned in your doctrinal beliefs?
- Are they flexible to grow and change in areas that need growth and transformation?

These questions are important because they will probably have picked up some family practices or traits that you'll need to be aware of and possibly deal with during your courtship. Some of these practices may be spiritual in nature, and if not dealt with properly will turn out to be a thorn in your flesh during marriage.

In some families, anything spiritual goes, and they may assert that all roads lead to God. As such, witchcraft, New Age, and other similar cultic practices have become normalized. Unfortunately, unless they demonstrate a clear testimony of salvation, children growing up in these families are unlikely to know any better. And it's possible that you may run into someone from such a background who wants a serious relationship with you.

In other families, it may be normal for the husband to beat his wife. So, if you're in a relationship with someone with such a background, you must find a way to deal with such a fundamental difference before you continue with the relationship.

A harmless way of having a glimpse into these differences might be to talk about how your own parents relate with each other at home. After listening to you, they may volunteer to tell you about their own parents' family life. If they don't share, pray for wisdom on an appropriate way to ask an open-ended question about their family.

It is important that you're prayerful during this critical phase of your life. Pray for each other separately. Also, set aside time to regularly pray together as well. Consider combining fasting with your prayers for greater effectiveness. Remember, your prayerfulness shouldn't only be about their family background. It should be about everything regarding your relationship as a whole.

Cultural backgrounds

In our era of mass movement of people around the globe, meeting people from a different cultural background is a reality that no one should ignore. Certain cultural beliefs or practices are normal for people from some backgrounds while they may be strange to yours. Many of those cultural practices are going to be beautiful and exciting, but others may seem both strange and shocking at the same time.

For example, in some cultures it's normal to marry more than one wife. Of course, we know that such a practice is legally forbidden in Judeo-Christian societies such as Canada. Unfortunately, some people still find ways around it. Or if they elect to go back to their country of birth at some point, you may have to follow them and will become immersed into their original culture. Check into what different practices may exist and thoroughly investigate if they accept them and their reasoning for adhering to the customs. Make sure you do the research before you proceed further with the relationship.

In some cultures, women are treated like they are subhuman or even as household objects with little or no respect, while men are treated like kings. Even though Christian values and Canadian civil laws abhor such behaviours, some people with similar cultural backgrounds still manage to practice this type of lifestyle with their wives being silent or too scared to speak up.

> *Check into what different practices may exist and thoroughly investigate if they accepts them and their reasoning for adhering to these customs. Make sure you do the research before you proceed further with the relationship.*

Differences in financial values

Having interacted with many couples from different backgrounds, I have concluded that money is one of the leading causes of marriage breakdown. But don't take my word for it. Goldhart & Associates, a Toronto based family law firm has also come to that conclusion. I think almost anyone who has either counselled couples who have a troubled marriage, or is divorced will agree that money is often part of the problem. Sometimes the affected couple may not be blunt about saying money was the issue; however, when you listen to them carefully and long enough, the money factor as the root cause of their problem will become evident.

Therefore, it would be beneficial to lookout for potential differences concerning finances early. Some areas to watch out for are the following: are they generous or tight-fisted? Are they selfish? If you're a generous person and they are stingy, you're likely to end up with conflicts. For example, you may want to give to meet a need while they may prefer that you first meet their personal need instead.

I have heard some spouses wonder what in the world is wrong with their partner since they're busy giving to outsiders while there're obvious and pressing needs in their immediate family. Some have gone to the extent of blackmailing their spouse that they're trying to create a false impression to outsiders that they are doing well when the reality is that they have bigger needs at home.

> *Having interacted with many couples from different backgrounds, I have concluded that money is one of the leading causes of marriage breakdown.*

The partner may argue that as far as they are concerned, it's hypocritical to help others when you're unable to meet your own household needs. But we know that you don't have to solve all your immediate and personal problems before you can help others. Sometimes, when you give to others who are in need, you're sowing seeds and soon enough, you'll reap a bumper harvest that'll lead to the solution you might have been looking for.

As Christians, we're called into a life of generosity and selflessness. A good perspective to hold is that giving from a Christian perspective is to give in love to meet someone else's need. But it's good to also understand that giving is an act of sowing. A farmer doesn't only sow a seed because they don't have anything else to do with the seed, nor do they scratch their head and ask, "Oh what am I going to do with the excess of seeds that I have?" before proceeding to sow. Sowing is always an intentional and thoughtful act. A farmer sows because they know that it is a wise thing to do. They sow in faith eagerly anticipating that they will harvest much more than the seed they've sown. Jesus taught that when we give it'll be given to us in return (Luke 6:38).

> *A farmer doesn't only sow a seed because they don't have anything else to do with the seed.*

Sometimes, generosity will demand that you give while overlooking your personal or family need. A great example of this kind of sacrificial giving is the familiar story of the widow of Zarephath which is found in 1 Kings 17:9-24. This widow sowed by giving the prophet Elijah what she clearly referred to as her last meal, which she had planned to eat with her son and then die.

The moment she released what she described as a handful of flour in a bin, and a little oil in a jar as a seed, her miracle began. Her handful of flour and a little oil kept on multiplying, meal after meal, and day after day. She fed herself, her son, and prophet Elijah throughout the duration of the famine. Generosity is a kingdom principle that has never failed. It's simply impossible for anyone to be wrong for being generous.

> *Generosity is a kingdom principle that has never failed.*

Frivolous Spending

I had an opportunity to talk to a couple whose main problem was that the wife spends uncontrollably and frivolously. The husband complained that as soon as money came into their joint account, his impulsive shopper-wife would go on a shopping spree until the account returned to a zero balance. She would buy both things they needed and things they didn't need. The husband complained that his wife didn't have any sense of priority. According to him, that lifestyle was taking a toll on their marriage. If you're observant, you will be able to pick up on such a tendency if it exists early in the relationship.

Here are some questions to help you determine your partners attitude to money.

Are they a faithful giver?

General giving and tithing are a fundamental indication where a believer stands with his or her financial resources. I've found these to be the best way to gauge a believer's attitude toward money. General giving and tithing are practical things. You either give or you don't. Therefore, don't let them get verbose about how wonderful givers they are. Let their record of giving speak for itself.

Are they willing to delay personal gratification to help someone in need?

Are they kind-hearted and incapable of closing their eyes to someone in need?

Are they willing to make financial plans as a family and stick to that plan?

You stand a better chance of succeeding when you make plans. Planning your finances together is a good indication that you are prepared to work in agreement for the good of the family. With agreement and careful planning, you'll accomplish a lot together as a couple.

> *For which of you, intending to build a tower, does not sit down first and count the cost, whether he has enough to finish it—lest, after he has laid the foundation, and is not able to finish, all who see it begin to mock him, saying, 'This man began to build and was not able to finish?' (Luke 14:28–30 NKJV)*

Are they able to distinguish between a need and a want?

Depending on how much money is available, buying what you want as opposed to what you need may lead to frivolous spending.

What are their financial liabilities?

How much consumable debt are they carrying? How many credit cards and lines of credit do they have? Even more important, are there balances on those credit cards and lines of credit? In general, a heavy consumer debt load shines a bright light onto someone's poor spending habits. Manageable debt load is fine. And spending within one's means is a good place to be. As a Christian, ultimately aiming to be free of debt is the ideal place to be.

These questions are only a guide for you to gain a sneak peek into the attitude of the person you're dating toward money. It's not a basis to be judgmental. Maybe your background has helped you to be more grounded in some of these topics than them. Therefore, if they are teachable and growth-oriented, you should welcome the opportunity to become the "iron that will sharpen them".

How to Handle Differences

Let me assure you that there are some ways to handle differences without splitting as a couple. There are some effective means of compromising that honour your differences, and the outcome could turn out to be so much fun for both of you.

A friend recently told me a story of a young biracial couple who managed their differences this way. The wife was from a West African country while her husband was a white Canadian. She married not knowing that camping was a big deal to her husband and a tradition of his. She on the other hand disliked bugs, mosquitoes, and the lack of running water; all of which are often associated with camping. As a result, she did not find those kinds of outdoor adventures to be fun. To manage their differences in this area, they resolved that whenever the husband would go on his annual camping trip with his birth family, she would go and spend time with her parents.

As Christians, we need to be practical during the days of courtship to try and understand the hobbies and interests of the other person, and then find effective ways to manage any differences that may arise. Being able to detect the differences that I've described above is a great starting point. However, of even greater importance is to come up with a plan to deal with the differences. Ideally, the plan should be made when the difference is identified, and the detection may happen during the courtship period. But if you both missed the difference during your courtship and you are now married, you can still maturely craft a plan on how to deal with it.

First, both individuals should be open about who they really are instead of concealing any weakness or poor character traits. Just be yourself. There's no need to pretend to be someone you aren't. Transparency is important in building trust, and trust is necessary for building a solid, healthy, and enduring marriage.

> *Transparency is important in building trust, and trust is necessary for building a solid, healthy, and enduring marriage.*

Therefore, it's important to point out the differences as they are discovered. It won't be helpful to overlook or pretend that the differences don't matter. Perhaps, it may not matter during your courtship because you'll still be in the euphoria of being in love. But don't be fooled! It won't be too long before you will realize that the differences have suddenly become sore points in your marriage. For that reason, it's advisable to save yourself the grief of dealing with conflicts later that should have been dealt with during the courtship.

It'll be more beneficial for your long-term relationship if you can project yourself into how you will handle such situations in marriage if they were to occur. If you sense the differences during courtship, they'll most likely show up during marriage. For that reason, being transparent about your real personality, family, cultural beliefs, social, and financial values and then finding ways to deal with the differences early on while dating will be invaluable when going into marriage.

> *Therefore, being transparent about your real personality, family, cultural beliefs, social, and financial values and then finding ways to deal with the differences early on while dating will be invaluable when going into marriage.*

You'd never forget that courtship is the ideal period for mutual discovery and transparency is an important key in that process. Therefore, you must be willing and comfortable to discuss issues and come up with a joint resolution plans.

> *Differences in themselves are not a bad thing, but not dealing with them will be detrimental to the relationship in the long run.*

Your ability to work together to resolve differences that you have identified during the dating period is significant because this will give you some experience in your ability to manage the relationship. Again, do not put a lid on any issues. Make sure you're satisfied that the differences have been dealt with. It isn't helpful to pretend that the differences no longer exist when they do. Do not ignore your differences.

Set and Respect Boundaries

One thing to always keep in mind is that whenever God tells us not to do something it's because he has a better plan that's ultimately for our good. That plan is based on his amazing and unconditional love for us. He tells us in Jeremiah, "For I know the thoughts that I think toward you, says the Lord, thoughts of peace and not of evil, to give you a future and a hope." (Jeremiah 29:11 NKJV). God's main plan is to make sure that we don't get hurt by following our own imperfect paths.

Boundaries refer to the limits you mutually agree that should be in place to protect both your individual and well-being of your relationship. For Christian singles who are courting, boundaries are important because they help to determine what you can and cannot do prior to getting married. Not setting boundaries or failing to guard against breaking them can hurt both the relationship as well as you, personally. For example, cohabiting relationships have shown to be unstable as the commitment in them is rarely close to what usually characterizes those of properly married couples. So, when you engage in cohabitating it may not end well, which results in those involved being hurt.

How to Initiate Boundaries

As a man, you should exercise your leadership role to lead your fiancée in setting boundaries and guarding each other against breaking them. That way, you both will understand each other's expectations. These boundaries should become a guide for you both as the relationship develops. Some of the boundaries may outlive the courtship period. Be proactive and set these boundaries in the relationship as early as possible.

Once the boundaries are put in place, you must both be accountable to each other in ensuring that they are maintained throughout the period of the courtship. There's a saying that it takes two to tango. It's going to take both of you to either maintain or violate the boundaries that you've set for yourselves. We will discuss some examples of typical boundaries that Christian singles in courtship should discuss and include in their relationship.

Sexual intimacy

Some singles who are courting with the intention to get married argue that it's perfectly normal to enjoy sexual intimacy before marriage. The good news is that most people still believe that premarital sex or sex outside of marriage is not the right thing to do. As a couple who love themselves, it's important to resolve between yourselves that there will be no sexual intimacy until after your wedding ceremony.

Perhaps most people ordinarily will not fall into the temptation of sexual intimacy if they're wise and proactive enough to take the necessary precautions. The first and most important precaution is to discuss it early and commit between yourselves that you'll do everything that is necessary to avoid it. Another important precaution to take is to avoid being alone in tempting circumstances, such as spending nights together. If you are going to be together in a tempting environment, it'll be good to invite your Christian brothers or sisters into the boundaries and standards you have set in your relationship so that they can encourage you and keep you accountable.

Cohabitation

Cohabitation can be described as a state of living together and having a sexual relationship without being married.

Sadly, it's becoming more prevalent these days and many unmarried people see it as normal and acceptable. Cohabitation cannot be considered normal and acceptable. What is wrong remains wrong no matter how prevalent or widely accepted it becomes. The couple must first decide that cohabitation will never be an option and that they won't live together under any circumstance until they are married.

> *What is wrong remains wrong no matter how prevalent or widely accepted it becomes.*

Beth a member of my church recently told me a story about her niece Amy, who demonstrated how valuable and principled she was to her boyfriend. Amy had dated her boyfriend for about twelve years. For more than half of that period, Josh her boyfriend put immense pressure on her to move in with him, so they could start living together. Amy would simply tell Josh that she was sorry but she couldn't move in with him until they were married. By the end of their thirteenth-year of dating, she told Josh that it was clear to her that he was wasting her time. With that statement, they broke off the relationship. Clearly, Amy demonstrated to Josh that she wasn't that kind of girl who would cohabitate. Never!

Some of the singles who are cohabiting or are contemplating it have asked what's wrong with it. Everyone is doing it these days. My standard answer to that question is "Oh I see! But since when did you change your name to 'Everyone'? You're certainly not 'Everyone'." I continue by letting them know that they've a unique identity as a child of God. I usually nicely suggest to these singles that perhaps they need to grow up a little bit more, because being a copycat simply means that they don't have a mind of their own, especially when you are caught doing something simply because others are doing it.

I also ask those arguing in favour of cohabiting to double check the identity of the crowd that is cohabiting. Who are they? Are they Christians like you? Do they know what you have been privileged to know? Do they have a similar upbringing as you? If they aren't, and don't, why are you allowing those who don't have a similar background to set an example for you?

Alcohol consumption

I have heard some people argue that alcohol consumption is a matter of conviction. Those who drink have suggested that they see nothing wrong with consuming alcohol. But those who don't believe that alcohol consumption is good for their physical and spiritual health can add alcohol avoidance to their list of boundaries that they may set for themselves. Whatever your decision on this topic may be, it'll likely become an ethical standard for your family after marriage. If you chose to consume alcohol during courtship, you may well continue consuming it into your married life and vice versa.

Physical contact and kissing

In general, appropriate physical contact is normal as it's a good way of showing love and care. This may include hugging and holding hands. But any contact that may lead to sexual arousal must be avoided. I've also heard some young people mention that they avoided kissing throughout their courtship period. They proudly testified that their first kiss was the bridal kiss on their wedding day. When pressed to explain why they avoided kissing during their courtship, they explained that it was their modest effort to avoid anything that would potentially lead them into a grave temptation.

For those Already Married

Perhaps, you're already married, and the concept of setting boundaries wasn't known to you during your courtship period. As such, you neither set any for yourselves nor maintained any. I will counsel that you should not allow yourself to be held captive by your past.

Here is what the Bible says about the infinite grace of God regarding you or any of his children who has fallen below his standards:

For a righteous man may fall seven times
And rise again, But the wicked shall fall by
calamity. (Proverbs 24:16 NKJV)

Lord, who is a God like you? You forgive sin.
You forgive your people when they do what is wrong.
You don't stay angry forever. Instead, you take delight
in showing your faithful love to them. Once again you
will show loving concern for us. You will completely wipe
out the evil things we've done. You will throw all our
sins into the bottom of the sea. (Micah 7:18-19 NIRV)

For I will be merciful to their unrighteousness, and their sins and their lawless deeds I will remember no more. (Hebrews 8:12 NKJV)

For the Lord your God is gracious and merciful, and will not turn His face from you if you return to Him. (2 Chronicles 30:9b NKJV)

He has removed our sins from us. He has removed them as far as the east is from the west. (Psalms 103:12 NIRV)

If we confess our sins, He is faithful and just to forgive us our sins and to cleanse us from all unrighteousness. (1 John 1:9 NKJV)

Our Heavenly Father is faithful and just, and his steadfast love for us is forever. It can't be exhausted. He's separated our sins from us even as far as the two farthest ends of the earth. Therefore, do not allow your past to define your life and your marriage. If God has forgiven you, you remain forgiven because God has no record of any of your past failures. Let me invite you to quit living in your past, which you may not have been so proud about.

However, if your conscience still haunts you, then make sure that you settle it with God and lean on the Holy Spirit to help deliver you from your past. You cannot change your past. But the good news is that you can determine how you want to live your life today and into the future. The present and the future are within your control. Therefore, take charge of your life and resist the baseless accusations of the enemy.

KEY TAKE AWAY

- Courtship is the period of mutual discovery for individuals who are dating for the purpose of marriage.
- Both individuals can get to know each other better by studying their personalities, family, spiritual beliefs, and cultural backgrounds.
- Differences are a good thing if they help you strengthen each other.
- People who are courting should set boundaries for themselves that will guide them in a morally upright relationship.
- Set up boundaries to ensure you are protecting yourselves and your relationship.
- Cohabitation and sexual intimacy are some of the boundaries that you should set for yourselves.
- You cannot change your past, but you can change your present and your future. Your present and the future are within your control.

CHAPTER FIVE

LISTEN TO TRUSTED ADULTS

When you're newly in love, you might feel like nothing else matters. Once you're committed, you realize that everything matters. Initially, you might not care that your dad doesn't approve of your partner. What does it matter when you're the one dating them? But over time, this small rift will affect your life and your relationship. If your family and friends don't like your partner, where is your support system? Will you be alienated from your friends and not invited to family events? Also remember that your family and friends know you best, and if they think there's a problem with your relationship, maybe you should listen.—Allison Renner

Make sure that you're taking full advantage of every opportunity that's available to you to get the relationship right. It would be wise to listen to what the trusted adults in your life have to say about your relationship. These adults may be your parents, spiritual mentors such as your pastor, or other well-regarded adults in your church community who know you well. As Allison Renner stated above, such perspectives may be invaluable because they're the people who will most likely be objective, which makes them well-positioned to see what you may not be able to see.

Why Should You Listen to These Views

These views may be invaluable because, most likely these people have your best interest and overall well-being at heart. Young people should especially note that your parents are the most excited people about your relationship besides yourself. Most parents look forward to the day when their son or daughter will get married. Therefore, they have nothing to gain from discouraging you from going ahead if indeed the relationship looks healthy and promising. But they have every reason to worry if the relationship doesn't look or feel right to them. Usually, such trusted adults will give cogent reasons why they feel apprehensive about your relationship. For that reason, it would be in your best interest to dispassionately consider their reasons.

Many people ignorantly argue that the choice of a life partner is strictly theirs, and their choice of whom to marry shouldn't be anybody's business. They say this to shut everybody out altogether. Yes, you're the one who's going to marry that person. However, unless the person you're marrying is an angel, you're most likely going to need some support along the way. That's where trusted adults such as parents will become handy.

Another risk of being adamant about your choice of whom to marry is in the event that you do have some struggles in your marriage, you may not be comfortable to go to your parents for guidance when you need it. I know a few cases where the couple decided that they would keep their struggles to themselves and create an impression that everything was just fine. Even when some think about approaching their parents for help, their conscience may convince them to shut up and live with the consequences of their choice.

For that reason, I'll suggest that shutting out the opinions of your trusted family members would be ill-advised! The reality is that your loving parents are just as interested in your happiness and you having a blissful marriage as you. I also think that most pastors like to see the marriages in their church thrive. Depending on how well the pastor who joined you knows you, they may equally feel bad if the marriage wobbles or falls apart at some point.

> *Many people ignorantly argue that the choice of a life partner is strictly theirs, and their choice of whom to marry shouldn't be anybody's business.*

I believe that if some of the young people had realized how much a struggling or failed marriage would affect their parents and others who love them, they would be more attentive to their dissenting views. I've watched parents languish in pain when their children's marriages fell apart. Therefore, if parents are saying that they have some misgivings about your relationship, it would serve you well to kindly pay attention.

After all, you trust those adults for a reason. To qualify to speak into your life, such people must have earned your trust long before you started your relationship. They may also have shown that they have acquired wisdom that comes through age and experience. While age doesn't always determine one's wisdom, there are important things an older person is more likely to see with greater ease than a younger person.

Who Should You Listen To

In addition, unlike you, who is directly involved in the relationship, a trusted neutral adult who is familiar with the relationship such as your parents or your pastor isn't emotionally involved to the same extent as you. Consequently, they're better able to see and provide a more objective counsel about the relationship. There is an ancient saying that states "what an older person may see sitting down, a younger person may need to stand on a fifty-thousand-foot elevation to be able to see it." What this adage means is that an experienced older person may easily see something long before it actually happens, whereas a younger person who is lacking experience may not see until after it happens.

> *What an older person may see sitting down, a younger person may need to stand on a fifty-thousand-foot elevation to be able to see it.*

I have had opportunities to keep close company with many mature and family-oriented Christian leaders since the early days of my work with the Lord. Those associations gave me a rare opportunity to learn some of the nuggets I've shared in this book. However, I must acknowledge with a great sense of gratitude that the Holy Spirit has also taught me a lot along the way. I've also learned many of these things by staying married to the right woman for more than twenty-five years. I can say with confidence that the experience and wisdom that come with age still counts.

Furthermore, I'll advise that no one should willfully ignore what the Bible also says in Proverbs 24:6: "For by wise counsel you will wage your own war, And in a multitude of counsellors there is safety." Don't discount it if such experience and wisdom are available to you. Take them to heart and put them to good use.

> *Remember that your family and friends know you best, and if they think there's a problem with your relationship, maybe you should listen.*

Obviously, the assumption here is that your parents are believers and have earned your trust over time. However, if they aren't believers and you do not trust them enough to give you sound guidance, then of course it would be safer for you to ignore their views about your relationship. Hopefully, you still have other trusted adults outside your immediate family who genuinely care about your well-being and may be able to speak into your life and your relationship. You'd count yourself blessed to have such people in your life.

A few years ago, Autumn a lovely and kind-hearted lady who was close to me met Jared online. They started a relationship that curiously grew very rapidly within a span of eight weeks. Most of their communication was in written format, but they also spent quite a bit time on the phone as well. Autumn was a senior citizen with adult children and grandchildren, but she clearly was nearly consumed by her relationship with Jared.

Because she trusted me, Autumn decided to share her seemingly burgeoning love relationship with me. With uncontrollable excitement, she compiled and forwarded me all her communication thread with Jared. In fact, by this time Jared had already confirmed plans to visit her. He asked her to wire him money so that he could pay for his flight from South Africa to visit her in Yellowknife, Canada. Once I went through their emails and chat threads, I immediately became suspicious.

As is the case with many relationships of this nature, Autumn was unable to discern the obvious red flags that were coming from Jared. I did an online search about him and based on his online footprint I was able show Autumn that his story was replete with gross inconsistencies. Everything about him, from his physical location, professional background and employment, his past family life, and how much he was worth embodied inconsistency. I knew that this must be one of those fake individuals preying on innocent ladies who are honestly looking for a relationship.

To further confirm my suspicion about the fellow, I suggested some questions that Autumn should ask him. Once he was confronted with those questions, he went on the defensive. He wondered why Autumn was suddenly asking him such probing questions. When it became obvious that he'd been caught, he stopped communicating with Autumn. And that was the end of the relationship.

To Autumn's credit, she understood the value of sharing such a personal experience with a trusted neutral person. Fortunately for her, I helped her to identify the internet scammer that Jared was, leading to a good end for her.

> *I knew that this must be one of those fake individuals preying on innocent ladies who are honestly looking for a relationship.*

KEY TAKE AWAY

- Trusted adults who express misgivings about your relationship are likely to be doing so because they love you.
- Trusted adults have a genuine interest in your well-being. Listen to what they have to say about your relationship. You'll be happy that you did.
- It's ill-advised to suggest that nobody should tell you how they feel about your relationship. Saying this means that you're asking people who care deeply to stop thinking about your overall well-being.
- Wise counsel from experienced adults is a pathway to safety.
- It a privilege and blessing to have trusted adults who are experienced, mature with the wisdom and have the courage to speak into your life.
- You'll want to keep your trusted parents and other adults in your relationship as you may need them down the road.

CHAPTER SIX

TOUGH TOPICS

There are certain things an average couple will have to contend with as an integral part of their married life. Almost every couple will have to deal with money, children, household chores, career, and more. More-often-than-not, these things tend to bring conflict in marriages. In this chapter, I will discuss these four important topics that often impact marital relationships, and I will suggest how intending couples could handle them.

Money

There's probably no one who doesn't know that money is a good thing. In fact, he who has money possesses a very good thing. With money you can acquire the necessities of life. And if you have lots of it, it can buy you many luxuries as well. Also, the more money you have the greater the number of friends you will have. Proverbs 19:4 says, "Wealth makes many friends, But the poor is separated from his friends." Furthermore, with money you can have a great deal of influence because money positions you to do many things. Often, money will open doors that might otherwise remain securely shut. It is, therefore, no surprise that the Bible says money answers all things (Ecclesiastes 10:19).

But in another twist, the Bible says that the love of money is the root of all evil (1 Timothy 6:10). It's important to understand that money itself is not responsible for all the evil that we see in our world today. Money can be used for worthy causes. It is one's attitude towards money—and what money is used to achieve—that will reveal whether it is a worthy possession or a bastion of evil.

Unfortunately, there's an abundance of evidence that the negative influence money tends to have on some people sometimes finds its way into marriages as well. This ought not to be so! For example, Sarah was in a well-paying job with an upstream oil and gas company. She fell in love with Chris, and they got married. Chris was not as lucky in holding down a good job. He was in and out of low wage jobs most of the time. Sarah was for the most part the main wage earner and she was paying for their livelihood. As a result, she showed little to no regard for her husband, regularly demeaning him by telling him how worthless he was. She often would ask him, "What man sits to be fed by his wife? I pay our mortgage, groceries, and everything else. If not for me, you'd be on the street." On several occasions she told Chris, "You aren't worthy being my husband. We aren't in the same class." Unfortunately, their marriage did not last longer than six years before they separated.

> *Unfortunately, there is an abundance of evidence that the influence-peddling nature of money often finds its way into marriages.*

To make sure that money only serves as an instrument for building strong, high-functioning, and enduring marriages, a couple who is courting should discuss money openly and thoroughly before they wed. It is crucial for the couple to discuss it honestly.

Many people think that if they're too forthright about matters such as money during their dating period, they'll turn their partner off. As a result, they end up playing it safe just so they can get through the courtship phase. Sadly, not long after the wedding, money and some of the other things they avoided discussing will surface and start to rock the marriage. For these couples, by not talking openly before the wedding they only postponed the inevitable unhappy marriage, big blowouts, or even divorce.

> *To make sure that money only serves as an instrument for building strong, high-functioning, and enduring marriages, the courting couple should discuss money openly and thoroughly before they wed.*

I would discourage intending couples from avoiding or postponing discussions about money until after the wedding. You probably do so at the peril of your marriage.

Expectations about money

Quite often, people who are courting assume that they have common expectations about money. Unfortunately, soon after their wedding they shockingly discover that they aren't aligned in their understanding and expectations. The courtship period is the best time to discuss and decide on important money-related topics such as having a joint bank account or not.

Adrienne was the owner of a successful mid-size technology firm within Canada's Silicon Valley region. Her partner, Keith was a director of innovation at a research firm in the Greater Toronto Area. The pair courted boisterously for a little over one year. Then, they hosted a beautiful wedding that attracted a large gathering of friends and family.

Keith had assumed that once they got married, Adrienne would add him to all her personal and company's bank accounts, and he would become a joint signatory. Adrienne, on the other hand was expecting that Keith would hand over all his bank accounts to her. In fact, they both took it for granted that once they married their spouse's money will automatically be theirs. Interestingly, they kept those lofty expectations to themselves. Neither of them brought these expectations up for discussion. They simply took it for granted that what they expected was going to be the natural thing to happen.

Within months after their wedding, they discovered there was a huge misalignment in what they were expecting from each other in terms of having unrestricted access to each other's money. Adrienne felt it was not a wise thing to operate a joint account with Keith. Keith, on the other hand believed that his wife was rich and shouldn't be expecting any money from him. As a result, tension started mounting between them.

Keith would say to Adrienne, "You're my wife. You're supposed to give me your money. What kind of wife holds onto and claims personal ownership of her money?" Adrienne in response would tell Keith to grow up and start being a man who looked after his family. She'd ask Keith to give her money for everything in the house because she was his wife. She'd remind him, "You're the head of the family. Perform your primary responsibility of providing for your family." More than once, as Keith narrated his marital ordeal, Adrienne quoted 1 Timothy 5:8 to support her position, which she held onto so tightly. That passage says, "But if any provide not for his own, and especially for those of his own house, he has denied the faith and is worse than an infidel."

> *Quite often, people who are dating sometimes assume that they have common expectations about money. Unfortunately, soon after their wedding, they shockingly discover they were miles apart in their understanding and expectations.*

Beginning with their conflict about money, needless disagreements started brewing in other areas of their family life. And sadly, things got out of hand. Approximately eighteen months after their wedding they went their separate ways and eventually filed for divorce. This example illustrates that it'll serve any intending couple well if they can bring up their expectations about money and discuss the topic as an important part of their courtship phase.

Dating is also the right time for a couple to make a commitment to each other that they won't operate a secret bank account. A secret bank account is when a spouse sets up an account that the other spouse is not aware of. Increasingly, couples are agreeing to the idea of having a joint bank account these days. Unfortunately, some go behind their spouse's backs and set up bank accounts for only themselves. Many who have done this have confessed to feeling that they've lost control of their finances, which they were used to prior to getting married. Sadly, the issue of secret accounts seem to becoming common among couples these days.

I'll admit that the church seems be divided on the issue of a couple operating a joint account. Majority strongly recommend that it is important for couples to have a joint account. And others recommend it's something that should be thoughtfully considered and agreed upon only by the couple themselves; that way, the couple can be committed to their choice with their whole heart. It usually is very awkward and even disappointing to be found to have a secret account when you're supposed to have an account that contains your joint earnings with your spouse. A secret account will with absolute certainty create doubt about money and will weaken your marriage in many ways.

The two most important points that I'll emphasize here are, first, if you agree that the idea of a joint account sounds good to you, then make sure all your money will be in that account. And second, every couple should determine and commit very early on that they'll never allow money to destroy their marriage. And they'd be accountable to each other in keeping this commitment.

> *It usually is very awkward and even disappointing to be found to have a secret account when you're supposed to have an account that contains your joint earnings with your spouse.*

Trust and transparency

Most of us will completely agree with the statement that there can't be an enduring relationship without trust. Trust is the linchpin that holds any meaningful relationship together. It is also true that trust must be earned. It can't be received on a golden plater. In other words, you must be intentional and work hard to earn your partner's trust. Also, it's important to keep in mind that trust will be tested so many times and in different scenarios during a relationship. That's why in a relationship no one can simply say, "But I am John, or I am Allison, therefore trust me." No! There's absolutely nothing about your name that it should form the basis for someone to trust you. If you want your partner to trust you, then take the necessary steps and earn that trust.

> *Trust is the linchpin that holds any meaningful relationship together.*

For that reason, I'll recommend that trust and transparency be the guiding words between any intending couples. It's safe to say that people who aren't transparent around their finances are not likely to be transparent in other areas of their lives. Lack of transparency can quickly lead to mistrust. A life of "hide and seek" gives rise to mistrust. That's why a lack of transparency and broken trust are always found together.

Make no mistake. If your spouse doesn't trust you around money, it will be hard for them to trust you in other areas of your marital relationship too. And the risk of not earning the trust of your spouse is too high to be entertained, because marriage is a relationship that requires you to have full trust in your partner. Furthermore, if two people don't feel that they can trust one another, they'd probably be well-advised to re-evaluate their plan to marry, or at least get some serious premarital counselling before they proceed to say, "I do."

> *It's often disappointing to be found to have a secret account when you are supposed to have all your money shared with your spouse.*

Think about it for a moment. As humans, we naturally tend to hold back our trust when we have doubts or when we don't know somebody well enough. Isn't it obvious how unlikely it would be for someone to vouch for another person whom there are lots of unknowns? If you truly want your marriage to flourish and be highly functional, then the couple must become an "open book" to one another.

Let's look at this classic example between the Lord and Abraham. When the Lord had determined that he'd destroy Sodom and Gomorrah, he had this to say during his encounter with Abraham:

> ***Shall I hide from Abraham what I am doing . . . For I have known him****, in order that he may command his children and his household after him, that they keep the way of the Lord, to do righteousness and justice, that the Lord may bring to Abraham what He has spoken to him. (Genesis 18:17-19 NKJV) (Note bolded words are for discussion)*

Do you see the power of trust in the above passage? God is saying, look, I know what Abraham is capable of doing, and I trust him; and it is for that reason that I can't afford to hide what I am about to do from him. God was transparent with Abraham. And as we know, following that disclosure from God, though Abraham couldn't save the city of Sodom, he was able to save Lot and his household. Intending couples, you have a responsibility to let your partner say unequivocally that they know and trust you, and as such that they can't hide anything from you in good conscience.

In the spirit of transparency and at the appropriate stage of their relationship, the couple may choose to disclose to each other how much they earn even before they get married. To help them achieve this desired level of transparency in money matters, the couple should learn early to use the language of "us" instead of "me" or "I." Using the language of "us" will go a long way in helping to effortlessly change from a single to a couple's mindset.

Children

Behold, children are a heritage from the Lord, The fruit of the womb is a reward. Like arrows in the hand of a warrior, So are the children of one's youth. Happy is the man who has his quiver full of them . . . (Psalms 127:3–5 NKJV).

Most married couples usually look forward to having at least one child of their own, and most of us will agree that children are still one of the typical ways that people measure the blessing of their marriage union. As obvious as the topic of children is, many couples get married without first discussing how many children they'd like to have, or even if they'll have any children at all. As a result, some couples end up having arguments about the number of children that's right for them. Therefore, it's important to discuss this during the courtship phase of your relationship.

Dorothy had never married before and did not have any children. She married Boyd, who was marrying for the third time with a total of four children from his two previous marriages. With four children to his name, Boyd was no longer interested in having any more children. Unfortunately, this discussion did not come up in any of their conversations when they were courting.

After their wedding, Dorothy who already was in her mid thirties was eager to have a child. That was in a stark contrast to Boyd's expectations. He told Dorothy that he was not interested in having more children, and he added, the burden of raising the four he had was already taking a toll on him.

Dorothy asked him, "Why didn't you tell me this when we were courting?"

Boyd replied, "Why didn't you ask me what my expectations were about having more children? To be completely honest with you, my love, I thought you would be content being the mother of my four children." He disclosed his thoughts with a so-called honesty without thinking about the emotional impact on Dorothy.

> *Why didn't you ask me what my expectations were about having more children?*

"What a cruel thing to say to a woman. That's cruel!" Dorothy reacted. "Anyway, yes, I am happy to be the mother to your four children. But I also want to carry a pregnancy and have a child that I can truly call my own."

Boyd did everything he could to make sure that Dorothy didn't become pregnant. It took lots of talking and prayer support from friends before Boyd eventually agreed to have a child with Dorothy. Thankfully, their story ended much better than other similar tales. Dorothy is now a happy mother of a seven-year-old son.

> *Anyway, yes, I'm happy to be the mother of your four children. But I also want to have a child that I can truly call my own.*

Once again, you'll be well-advised to discuss your desire for children and even how many you'd like to have before marriage. As obvious as the issue of having children may seem to you, it may not be a priority to your fiancé or fiancée. Bring it up and discuss it. That way, you'll be on the same page before you wed.

Career

A career can be a make-or-break aspect of some people's lives. For some people they wouldn't trade their career for anything else, not even for their marriage. The thought of advancing up the corporate ladder, taking up new challenging responsibilities, and becoming powerful with the perks that go along with such positions means everything to them. And that's probably fine for them as there's nothing wrong about being carried away with one's career. Besides, that's who they are. It's an essential part of their personality.

> *The thought of advancing up the corporate ladder, taking up new challenging responsibilities, and becoming powerful with the perks that go along with such positions means everything to them.*

Experience has shown that some people's lives are defined by what they do and how much they earn. Therefore, don't assume anything or take anything for granted with the person you are dating when it comes to their work and career. Since you are still getting to know each other, you may not be aware that the person you are dating is one of those people whose job comes first before anything else. For that reason, the courtship period is the ideal time to discuss your career aspirations.

My beautiful sweetheart is a career-minded person, a fact I didn't know until after we were married and started having children. I had wrongly assumed that she'd be happy to be a stay-at-home mom and look after our children until at least they were old enough to start going to school. However, that was not the case. At that time, her salary was barely enough to even cover the high cost of daycare for our three children. I tried very hard to make her see that it made very little sense to be working just to pay the daycare operator. I expected her to realize that the quality time she'd be spending with our children alone was worth her sacrifice of being a stay-at-home mom. Unfortunately, I was not able to convince her.

Well, they say happy wife, happy life. So, I wholeheartedly supported her in her professional development and career. We were able to juggle our jobs with the childcare system until they had reached the age to be able to be home alone for a few hours after school until one of us got home to take care of them.

Well, they say happy wife, happy life.

Another example of career becoming an issue in a marriage is Fiona and Drew. Fiona was working for one of the world's big five oil and gas companies as a petrophysicist, while her husband Drew was a management accountant with a large accounting firm. Their marriage was six years old, and they had three children. Both Fiona and Drew were doing well in their jobs. Over the course of time, Fiona got offered a much sought-after three-year assignment in the North Sea.

Ordinarily, this type of assignment would have been a major highlight in Fiona's career. The total take home package was very attractive too. Too attractive for anyone to decline. But instead of the couple celebrating this important phase of their lives as a couple, the situation brought unbelievable tension into their marriage.

Drew was not keen having to resign his job and relocate to the North Sea with his wife. What will I be doing once I get there? Staying at home all-day, he asked himself repeatedly. Another ego driven thought also came into his head of whether he should be the one following Fiona up and down the countryside because of her job? There's no man who would do that, he concluded. However, letting Fiona go with the children while he stayed behind alone was not even to be contemplated.

Fiona tried to persuade her husband by asking him to reconsider the pay package that she had been offered. It was enough money for them to live very comfortably even if he wasn't working. Plus, the assignment would increase her chances of progression in her career. She also reminded Drew that this kind of opportunity wasn't available to everyone at her company, but was a special career opportunity for her.

With only three weeks until Fiona was to start her new role in faraway Aberdeen, the couple still hadn't agreed upon the best way to manage the situation. For Fiona, there was nothing to discuss as she was dead set on going. Drew, on the other hand hadn't seen how he would fit into Fiona's so-called once-in-a-lifetime international assignment. Fiona's parents tried unsuccessfully to convince their son-in-law of the job's advantages. Fiona's last effort was to talk to Drew's parents. That too, didn't yield any positive results.

Time almost was running out as Fiona had only two weeks left to report at her new job. The back and forth conversations on the best way to handle her husband's opposition had persisted. Meanwhile, all the travel arrangements had been made for Fiona and her family. Her employer was funding her entire relocation expenses, including those for her spouse and children. In the last seven days before her departure, they were both ready for a showdown. Drew told her that since he was the husband and the head of their home that he had spent enough time talking about this issue. He told her she had two clear choices, either her career or her family. He told her he wasn't following her to the North Sea. He advised that he needed her to let him know what her choice was in the next twenty-four hours.

Fiona was caught between a rock and a hard place. She cried her heart out. In the end, she opted for her career. Following her final decision to move to Aberdeen was the remaining question of how to manage her young children. She suggested that she would be going with her children, but Drew told her that she must be out of her mind to even mention taking his children along with her. The last week before she left for Aberdeen turned out to be the most difficult seven days of her life. She didn't have time to go to court where custody of the children could be determined. She had no other option but to leave her children with their dad.

That's why it's so important to discuss everything including career aspirations during courtship. There's no question that it's going to be a tough discussion to have, but it'll be safer to have the discussion ahead of exchanging vows. I don't think knowing where you both stand in terms of career aspiration would be enough reason to back out of the relationship. Therefore, don't be afraid of bringing it up for discussion. The key benefit of discussing this issue will be that you both become well-informed about each other's career aspirations. And beyond any doubt, having such knowledge about your prospective spouse can only be a good thing.

How to initiate a career-related conversation

Perhaps, you may be wondering how to initiate a conversation about the important topic of careers. Here is a short list of career-related questions or scenarios you may use to start a discussion during courtship:

- Your spouse has been transferred to another city, province, or state and relocation is required. What will be your reaction?
- In this era of globalization, it is possible that your spouse may get an international assignment that

will require them to relocate. Will you be flexible to follow your spouse on an out-of-country assignment? If not, how will you handle the situation? What will be your options?

- The nature of your spouse's job includes lots of travel, often involving several days away from home each month or even each week. What will be your disposition to such a work situation?
- You have started raising a young family. And daycare is not an attractive option to you as a couple for a variety of reasons. Will one of you be willing to put your career on hold and be the stay-at-home parent to look after the children until they have grown to a specific age?

Chores

One thing to keep in mind regarding household chores is that couples should avoid role delineation. Role delineation is where the couple insists that certain things must be done by the husband while certain tasks are strictly the wife's responsibility. Such a disposition can bring tension and stress into a marriage much sooner than the couple would realize.

For example, in some cultures it isn't common for a man to cook. In such cultures, all kitchen tasks are the exclusive responsibility of the wife. Luckily, in most of these cases, the cost of labour in those cultures is also affordable, which makes it easy to hire nannies and other domestic staff. As a result, the husband may get away with avoiding kitchen chores altogether.

But in other jurisdictions such as North America where the cost of labour is high, not many households can afford the luxury of hiring domestic staff. That leaves the husband with no choice but to step up and help with household chores. The husband should be able and willing to assist his wife with everything, including the kitchen chores. Nothing should stop the husband from going into the kitchen and cooking dinner for the family. There's nothing wrong for the husband to do dishes, take out the garbage, do laundry, and vacuum the floor. All these tasks should be discussed during courtship.

> *Nothing should stop the husband from going into the kitchen and cooking dinner for the family.*

Bryce and Aluemo were both young professionals and they both understood the importance of doing household chores together as a couple. Bryce grew up in a home where his father was an active helper of his mom. So, he picked up that strength from his father. Yes, helping your wife with household chores is a key strength for men.

Aluemo was the one who brought up the issue of household chores during their courtship. They discussed it, and Bryce readily agreed that he would be thrilled to help with cooking dinners every weekend. He also volunteered to be responsible for dishes Monday through Friday, the days when Aluemo would be cooking. They also agreed that they would always do grocery shopping together. Because they had this discussion before their wedding, the couple didn't have any issues with how the household chores would be tackled in their home.

It's important to always keep in mind that courtship is a period where you get to know your future partner. This is your opportunity to learn about them as much as possible. Use this time well and fully to achieve that goal. I believe that people who are in love should feel free to discuss anything and everything. Nothing should be considered silly or unnecessary. I find that discussing both the heavy topics and the seemingly trivial things adds fun to the whole courtship experience.

> *It's important to always keep in mind that, courtship is a period of getting to know your future partner.*

To some extent, surprises are good but only if they are pleasant and their impact is a positive experience. Otherwise, most people appreciate when they are given a heads-up regarding something that's about to happen. And discussions about these "Tough Topics" during courtship would eliminate or at least minimize the surprises that will come when you are confronted with difficult issues and topics for discussion as a married couple.

KEY TAKE AWAY

- Having money is important because it allows you to buy the essentials that make life easier. However, if not handled carefully and selflessly, money can damage relationships.
- Take time to have open conversations about money. Discuss important expectations such as operating a joint bank account or separate bank accounts and debt loads.
- Be sure to also discuss career aspirations, children, and household chore assignments.
- Building a high-functioning and long-lasting marriage requires transparency.
- Mistrust and lack of transparency are often found together.
- Discuss whether you both would like to have children or not. If you decide to be parents, you should also discuss the number of children you would like to have.
- Flexibility is strongly recommended as strict role delineation between partners often result in conflict.
- Don't be shy to discuss how household chores will be handled.

CHAPTER SEVEN

MARRIAGE VERSUS COHABITING

Marriage is God's beautiful idea. He conceived and took time to create it. God himself joined Adam and Eve as husband and wife. He intended that marriage be the foundation of the family. If we stick to God's original idea about family, we won't have all the different forms of families that exist in the world today. Examples of different family formats from what God intended are single parent households, cohabitation, common law partnerships, and so on. It's for this reason that I believe with all my heart that a family is best built upon marriage as its bedrock.

How it All Began

In Genesis, God said, "it is not good that the man should be alone; I will make him a helper comparable to him." (Genesis 2:18 NKJV). There are two key words in this important scripture to help us gain a better understanding of marriage. God, in his infinite wisdom decided that Adam and Eve needed to first be properly joined together in the institution of marriage. God officiated their wedding himself.

Let's try and understand this fascinating Bible verse. According to Genesis 1:31, prior to the creation of Eve, God saw everything he had made and declared that, indeed it was very good. However, one thing stood out as not being good. As shown in the first part of Genesis 2:18 above, the LORD said when he saw Adam all by himself that, "… it is not good that the man should be alone." Then God proceeded to provide a solution: "I will make him a 'helper comparable' to him." Eve was God's perfect solution to Adam's loneliness.

The word, "helper" as used in Genesis 2:18 above can best be understood through the Hebrew word, *ezer* which provides important information about the creation of Eve as the first woman. Ezer when translated means God was making Eve as Adam's "lifesaver." More than a dozen other uses of this word in the Bible refer to God himself. And it was used when the children of Israel needed God to come through for them under very desperate circumstances. For instance, in Deuteronomy, we've this verse, "There is no one like the God of Jeshurun, who rides on the heavens to help you…" (Deuteronomy 33:26 NKJV). This understanding reveals that God intended for Eve to be Adam's lifesaver, life giver, rescuer, or a strong and indispensable ally.

The second important Hebrew word in this verse, translated "comparable" is *kenegdo.* It literally means "according to the opposite of him." In other words, God's focus is on an appropriate match. Eve was not created above or below Adam; she was to complement Adam. The animals Adam had named each had an appropriate companion (Genesis 2:20), and Adam was given a fitting companion as well. Eve was "just right" for him.

Thus, when we combine these two words, you will appreciate the mindset of God about marriage. God was essentially saying that he would make for man a "helper comparable" that will be a lifesaver, an ally who will just be right for Adam. Therefore, we can safely state that the wife is such a critical part of her husband's life that while they both are alive she will be an indispensable partner to her husband. A partnership like no other, such that without her there will be a gaping void in the man's life.

> *Therefore, we can safely state that the wife is such a critical part of her husband's life that while they both are alive she is an indispensable partner to her husband.*

As it's evident in everything around us, whatever God creates is well-thought-out and perfect. That's why marriage as a product of God's creation is such an essential part of our human existence. Therefore, marriage isn't just a nice thing to do to show that you've become a responsible adult. Marriage is known to have important benefits at both the individual and societal levels.

Our knowledge-driven generation has accumulated evidence that in virtually every way that researchers of any relevant human endeavour can measure, married people do much better than the unmarried or divorced. They live longer, healthier, happier, sexier, and above all, more affluent lives. And it's important to stress that both men and women equally enjoy these key benefits that marriage offers.

> *Married people normally live longer, healthier, happier, sexier, and above all, more affluent lives.*

Unfortunately, those multiple corresponding studies have found that these great outcomes are only true with properly constituted marriages. Such studies have been able to clearly establish that cohabiting relationships don't produce the same results. And I don't think it's difficult to explain why that's the case.

Proverbs tells us, "He who finds a wife, finds a good thing, And obtains favor from the Lord." (Proverbs 18:22 NKJV). It is equally true that she who finds a husband finds a good thing and obtains favour from the Lord. The favour that comes with marriage is mutual after all because they've become "one flesh." One observation I'd like to share here is that I've not yet come across a cohabiting couple who are courageous enough to call themselves husband and wife. They usually call themselves partners. Could it be possible that they probably know that they aren't truly husband and wife?

Unfortunately, many young people in some parts of the developed world are increasingly showing a lack of interest in wholeheartedly committing to the beautiful institution of marriage. They think the process of getting properly married is an unnecessary burden that should be avoided. As a result, some are opting for cohabitation as a short cut or seemingly easier approach. They usually argue that they are already living together happily, so what else does society expect from them? They question if it is the wedding ceremony itself, to mark the official beginning of the relationship, that makes their relationship a marriage.

A young man once asked me, "My girlfriend and I have been living together for about three years. We even have a baby, isn't that good enough?"

I congratulated him for being a dad, but I quickly answered his question: "No! that's not good enough because you're not yet married. Living together and having a child is not what makes your union a marriage."

Of course, nobody will stop you from living together as friends. But even from the social point of view, your living together will not be recognized as a marriage. Such relationships are referred to as cohabitation. Here's what cohabitation means according to Wikipedia: "*It is an arrangement where two people are not married but live together. They are often involved in a romantic or sexually intimate relationship on a long-term or permanent basis.*"

> *Living together and having a child is not what makes your union a marriage.*

That's what it is. If you want to regard yourself as a married couple so that you can confidently call yourselves husband and wife, then take the steps to do it the right way. For example, you can call a government registry or social services office in the jurisdiction where you live to get the necessary information about how to legally get married. You'll be pleasantly surprised how straightforward it is to properly and legally get married. The process is not complicated at all.

Comparison Between Marriage and Cohabitation[2]

Sexual satisfaction

Despite the lurid Sex in the City marketing that promises singles erotic joys untold, both husbands and wives are more likely to report that they have an extremely satisfying sex life than singles or cohabitors. Certainly, married people are more likely to have a sex life. Married people are also more likely to report a highly satisfying sex life. Wives, for example, are almost twice as likely as divorced and never married women to have a sex life that both exists and is extremely satisfying emotionally. Contrary to popular belief men who have a wife, beat cohabitors by a wide margin: fifty percent of husbands joyfully report that sex with their wife is extremely satisfying physically compared with just twenty percent of cohabiting men.

Physical safety

Marriage lowers the risk that both men and women will become victims of violence, especially including domestic violence. Some American studies have found that single and divorced women were four to five times more likely to be victims of violence in any given year than wives. Single men were four times more likely to be violent-crime victims than husbands. Statistics also show that two-thirds of the violent acts against women were committed by intimate partners who weren't their husbands, but rather by boyfriends (whether cohabiting or not) or former husbands. It is also true that people who are cohabiting engage in more violence against each other than legally married spouses.

This situation could be due to several reasons. There's a commitment that comes with marriage that can hardly be found in cohabitation or any other form of intimate relationship. I believe that commitment is a natural restrainer from aggressive behaviour that could become physical. The rigorous process of getting married serves two main purposes. It's the proven way of testing the depth of a man's love for the woman he's about to marry. It takes a lot of love to be willing to go through such rigour. After investing so much time and energy to marry the love of your life, you should deeply cherish her and not want to hurt her for any reason.

As humans, we know that there's usually a direct relationship between the value we place on something and the effort we make in getting that thing. For example, no one jokes with their diamond or gold possessions because they are expensive and the process of mining them is also not easy. For that same reason, I'll counsel young men wanting to marry to see the effort they're putting into the relationship as a measure of how important the girl is to them.

As humans, we know that there's usually a direct relationship between the value we place on something and the effort we make in getting that thing.

I once knew Andrea who was in a relationship with Kyle. In less than one year after their relationship began, she started taking her personal effects and leaving them at Kyle's house. And by the fifteenth month of their relationship, Andrea had completed the piecemeal move of her belongings into Kyle's house. Then she declared that she and Kyle were "married." Expectedly, everyone in the family was deeply disappointed with her behaviour.

Sadly, it didn't take long before Kyle turned Andrea into a punching bag. Fighting was a routine that came to define their relationship. On many occasions, Kyle would beat Andrea and even ask her when she would be going back to her father's house because he didn't marry her. He also would tell her that she was the one who packed her suitcases and came to live with him.

What was responsible for that kind of behaviour? Kyle had little value for Andrea most probably because he didn't put in any meaningful effort to marry her. Gold occurs deep in the ground, and to get it you must spend a significant amount of resources to mine it. The same is true of marriage. You should treat your betrothed like gold. Show them in every way that you value them by cherishing them. Single ladies too should see themselves as being precious and deserving special treatment by the man who is going to marry them. Therefore, no girl should make herself look or feel cheap. If you feel cheap, that's the way you'd be treated by others.

> *Gold occurs deep in the ground. And to get it, you must spend a significant amount of resources to mine it.*

Riches and wealth accumulation

Marrying properly doesn't have to be a financial burden as some men tend to think these days. Neither is marriage just another consumption item on a man's monthly budget. On the contrary, married couples often become richer than cohabitors or singles. Research shows that married people not only make more money, but also manage money better and build more wealth together than either would alone. This fact confirms what the Bible says, "Two are better than one, Because they have a good reward for their labor." (Ecclesiastes 4:9 NKJV).

At comparable income levels, married people are less likely to experience or report "financial hardship" or trouble paying essential bills than single individuals. The longer people stay married, the more assets they're able to build together as a couple.

Regardless of how long a cohabiting relationship lasts, there's no relationship to wealth accumulation whatsoever. Here's why: for many cohabiting couples, the main thing that binds them together is that they are living in the same home. It is like such couples usually say, "we are not married per se. Our relationship is not formal, so why should we make long-term financial plans together?" Yes, for these reasons and more, cohabiting lacks the necessary motivation to truly make any long-term financial plans together.

Sexual fidelity

Marriage increases sexual fidelity. Some statistical research results have indicated that cohabiting men are four times more likely to cheat than husbands, and cohabiting women are eight times more likely to cheat than wives. And this is a simple puzzle to solve. Cohabiting doesn't demand the kind of commitment or loyalty that marriage demands. As stated above, cohabiting couples don't value each other at the same level as married couples mutually value themselves. Expressed quite simply, the bond that is necessary to sustain a marriage is often absent in cohabiting relationships.

In addition, cohabiting doesn't guarantee a stable, reliable, and long-lasting romantic relationship. The lady's feeling of insecurity that she might be kicked out makes cohabiting relationships so unstable and therefore, prone to infidelity. For example, an American study of romantic relationships found that just ten percent of cohabiting couples are still cohabiting after five years. And this is obviously due to the reasons stated above. By contrast, eighty percent of couples who are in their first marriage are still married five years later.

> *Cohabiting doesn't guarantee a stable, reliable, and long-lasting romantic relationship.*

Happiness and fulfillment

Overall, forty percent of married people, compared with approximately twenty-five percent of singles or cohabitors say they are "very happy" with life in general. Married people are also only about half as likely as singles or cohabitors to say they are unhappy with their lives. And here's why: in general, God has created us to be social beings who crave good, strong, and stable relationships that add value to our lives. Relationships with these characteristics make us feel desired, valued, fulfilled, and important. And there's no relationship that delivers these benefits better than marriage, hence, married couples report greater happiness than singles or cohabitors.

> *In general, God has created us to be social beings who crave good, strong, and stable relationships that add value to our lives.*

Are you currently cohabiting? Or have you been wondering if cohabiting is a good thing? I hope that these reasons have sufficiently unearth the ills of cohabitation while showing the compelling benefits of getting properly married. I also hope that it won't be difficult for you to make the right choice between the two from here on.

KEY TAKE AWAY

- Many studies have shown that the benefits of marriage far outweigh the life of a single.
- Married people tend to accumulate wealth and become more affluent over time than singles or those cohabiting.
- Cohabitation by its very nature is characteristically unstable and offers less happiness and fulfillment to those involved.
- Marriage can contribute to better overall health.
- Married people tend to be happier and more fulfilled than those cohabiting.
- Married people tend to have more satisfying sex lives than those cohabiting.
- Marriage is the most value-add relationship available to us humans.

CHAPTER EIGHT

BE OPEN TO THE POSSIBILITY OF A BREAKUP

Jennifer and Gary had been dating for about five years. Around their fifth anniversary of dating, Gary went down on his knee and popped the question in a perfectly arranged and hard-to-forget engagement ceremony. Behind them were copious fond memories of their relationship up to that point. Shortly after popping the question, they fixed their wedding day for twelve months out. The reception venue had been booked and fully paid for, and the rest of wedding plans were in top gear. At this stage of their relationship, Jennifer was head over heels and fully convinced that "the die was cast."

By this time in their relationship, they already had started establishing some family traditions. One of their traditions was to hang out together for dinner every Saturday. But on this particular Saturday evening, out of nowhere Gary told Jennifer, "Now that our wedding is only ten months away, I want you to move in with me. I will appreciate it if you can do this within the next four weeks." He continued, "after all, we're now engaged, our wedding date has also been fixed, so there is no reason why we should still be living apart." Then, he went on to further explain, "as you know the wedding is going to cost a lot of money. Therefore, it's only prudent for you to move in with me so that we could save the money you'll be paying for rent to pay for some of our wedding expenses."

Jennifer was so shocked by his suggestion and suddenly became cold with him. She wondered within herself where such twisted logic could be coming from. She managed to keep calm and quiet. But in her silence was profound confusion. After dinner, Gary dropped Jennifer off at her house, said good night, and then drove away.

A week later, it was their weekly dinner again when Gary asked Jennifer, "have you thought through my suggestion yet?"

Jennifer replied, "I am not sure where such a suggestion is coming from. Of course, you know that wouldn't be the right thing for us to do. Remember, we are believers. What I will suggest is that we can spend as much time together as possible. But I can't move in with you at this time because we are not yet married. True, we are engaged. But as you know quite well, engagement is different from marriage." She continued, "let's exercise a little patience, after all our wedding is less than ten months away and we both will live together happily ever after."

Gary didn't like what he heard from Jennifer at all. "That sounds preachy," he thought to himself.

> *True, we are engaged. But as you know quite well, engagement is different from marriage.*

Gary didn't say much again about the issue, and they continued to spend more time together. About three months after Gary first suggested that she should move in with him, Jennifer stopped over at his house unannounced as she had done countless times during their five-year relationship. Expectedly, they both had keys to each other's house. Behold, Gary was home, but the door was locked from the inside, and Jennifer couldn't open the door because the key was still in the lock.

"This is out of character for Gary to lock himself inside the house before bedtime. What could he be doing inside?" she wondered. Then she went back and sat in her car and waited patiently in Gary's driveway. After a few minutes she decided to call his phone, but Gary didn't answer. She repeated trying to call two more times with no answer from Gary.

"What is going on inside the house behind that locked door? Is he okay?" Jennifer questioned no one in particular.

> *But what is going on inside the house behind that locked door? Is he okay?"*

After about two hours it was beginning to get dark. Finally, Gary came out, and with him was a beautiful lady. A very awkward scene ensued. On seeing Jennifer's car, Gary started reacting in shame and embarrassment.

"Oh! my God," he exclaimed. "Jennifer, what are you doing here?" he asked. Jennifer was so upset that she couldn't utter a word. She drove home crying all the way.

After about an hour later, Gary called Jennifer. But before Jennifer could say anything, he began to blame her for refusing to move in with him.

He continued his excuse, "I have been under so much emotional pressure, that's why I welcomed my former girlfriend when she offered to pay a visit. All this is your fault! Most people who are engaged to marry always live together and then get married from there. But you refused to do it. You're the one who has put me in this mess." He went on and on in defence of himself and continued putting all the blame on Jennifer.

Jennifer was so devastated that she took some time off from work to reflect on what had just happened. She concluded that she must call off their wedding plans. Gary tried to beg her to forgive him. She assured him of her forgiveness but was firm that with what had just happened, there was no way she would go ahead with the wedding as planned.

She wondered to herself, "Our wedding was only about six months away, and Gary has done this to me. He's shredded my heart into tiny pieces. What can Gary ever do to regain my trust? If he can cheat on me in such a childish and scandalous way, how can I be sure he won't do it again after we are married?" Those questions dominated her thoughts for the next couple of weeks.

Finally, she made up her mind. "No! I can't marry Gary. Going ahead with this wedding would be putting my trust in the wrong person. He's wrecked my life, but it's safer for me to call it quits from here," she firmly concluded to herself. She called Gary and told him that it was over! No amount of begging by Gary was enough to save their relationship. And they broke up.

That was a dramatic and sad situation, wasn't it? Yes, Gary and Jennifer were very close to saying, "I do". Should she have gone ahead under such circumstances just because they had dated for five years with their wedding only a few months away? Would it be worth it to try? Jennifer hadn't expected that there would be anything possible that could have prevented her from marrying Gary. But when the unthinkable happened, she was able to take control of herself and make a firm decision not go ahead with the wedding. I think she made a wise decision.

How to Evaluate the Relationship

This example illustrates why it's important to constantly keep the main objective of courtship in view. To reiterate, courtship is to help you answer the following questions:

- Are we a good fit for each other or not?
- Is there anything that could happen during our relationship that might stop us from getting married?

As you begin to know more and more about your partner in courtship, you should be able to answer these questions with certainty. Let me stress yet again that it's important that both individuals can answer these questions individually with confidence.

The following questions would be a useful guide for concerned couples:

- Are you fully convinced that you know yourselves well?
- Can you describe with a fair degree of accuracy who your partner is?
- Can you trust your partner completely with your tender heart of love?
- What differences have you discovered about each of your personalities?
- Are the differences deal makers or deal breakers?
- If they're deal breaking differences, have you been able to resolve them to your mutual satisfaction?

Why Should You Evaluate the Relationship

I'm putting great emphasis on the need to evaluate the relationship because many people go into courtship as if it's already a done deal. Instead of paying close attention to the all-important process of mutual discovery, they start fantasizing about their wedding day and become oblivious to potential showstoppers. You'll be doing yourself a disservice having such a disposition.

It's fitting to say this as many times as possible: it's naïve to think that some of the differences that may exist during your courtship will simply go away after the wedding. They won't! Therefore, if you identify key differences that you're unable to sufficiently deal with, you should be courageous enough to discontinue the relationship.

Let me caution you here that there's a good chance the other partner may not see your point of view. As such, it becomes the only time that it's okay for people to seek to protect their self-interest, and not minding what the other person thinks or feels. Be willing to accept being called selfish if it comes to that. You must keep in mind that it may take only one of you to summon the courage and say that something is not right with the relationship, and you have to say that you are out of it. But you must be careful to let the other person know that your decision is being made out of genuine love and it will be mutually beneficial in the long run.

Therefore, if you identify key differences that you are unable to sufficiently deal with, then you should be courageous enough to discontinue the relationship.

Yes! In this situation, the other party doesn't have to see your point of view. Nor should you feel obligated to wait indefinitely for them to agree with you that breaking up is the right thing for both of you. Go ahead if you are fully persuaded that breaking up is the right thing to do!

I must stress this because often people who are dating may be tempted to say that they don't want to hurt the other person. Others might say that they don't want to be the one to initiate the breakup. But the point that isn't up for debate is that it only has to take one of you to initiate that necessary pause or breakup. If you don't act on your instincts or beliefs, there won't otherwise be one.

We all know that a breakup in any relationship can be painful, but it's still much better and emotionally safer to breakup a courtship or an engagement than it is to breakup a marriage. If you go ahead grudgingly with a courtship that has obvious red flags, it may even end in a more terrible heartache. I've spoken to enough divorced people to know how badly divorce or unhealthy marriages hurt people.

You must have the courage to take a step back and decide for yourself whether it's better and less stressful to handle a breakup of an engagement or for it to end in divorce. An important distinction to keep in mind is that ending or putting a pause on an engagement is not a divorce. Divorce only happens after marriage. And no one should get me wrong on this one. Engagements themselves are a serious commitment. However, *the commitment in an engagement isn't anywhere close to the commitment in a marriage.* This is true regardless of the perspective one may hold.

In 2019, a young couple who was engaged to be married demonstrated this rare courage and called off their engagement. My wife and I knew the parents of the couple well. It was in the summer of 2018 that the young couple announced their wedding plans, which followed several years of courtship. About six months before their wedding day, the couple announced their breakup and sent out an apology to the large number of guests who had been invited. They cited an irreconcilable difference between them as the reason for the breakup. Of course, people who knew them started to wonder if they didn't understand themselves well enough before they fixed a date for their wedding.

The couple must have understood themselves well enough to decide to fix a date for their wedding. But unfortunately, something came up that they mutually considered significant enough for them to cancel their wedding plans and to even breakup altogether. They demonstrated that though it hurts, it was better for them at that point to end things rather than go ahead despite what they eventually deemed to be "too significant" to overlook. They made the difficult decision because it was the safest choice for them to make.

Initially, it was a bit awkward in terms of the public perspective. But within weeks, those of us who had been on the guest list accepted their decision. They did the right thing because a failed engagement is far better than a failed marriage.

> *A failed engagement is far better than a failed marriage.*

A "Go or No Go" Decision

After a period of the engagement, there'll come a time when you'll need to make that most important decision, whether to ultimately proceed into marriage or not. I call this crucial decision a "Go or No Go" decision.

I liken it to the final investment decision, a term that is often used in capital project management. This is the decision period during which the contracts for all equipment can be placed, allowing procurement and construction to proceed and engineering to be completed. This judgment is usually made with a great deal of thought and considers every factor known and anticipated. Additionally, this decision is usually made with the mindset that going ahead with the project is the right thing to do. Once the decision to go ahead is made, there's usually no intention to back out.

Every person who is engaged to be married will have to make this decision at some point. I consider it to be critical and final because for a Christian, turning an engagement or proposal into a marriage should be understood as a lifelong undertaking. Yes, you must prayerfully consider all options before proceeding to tie the knot. It is true that the man most likely did pray before he got down on his knee to propose. And hopefully, although women are often caught unawares, she was praying all along that she would give the right answer whenever he would propose. But there is still some more praying to be done along the way. You still have an opportunity to back out of the relationship if there is a very good reason to do so, before you finally say, "I do." This option was illustrated in the example of Gary and Jennifer's story earlier in the chapter. By praying and by careful thought, you will know that you'll not begin to regret your decision to marry a few months or a few years down the road.

> *Therefore, you must prayerfully consider all options before proceeding to tie the knot.*

KEY TAKE AWAY

- Keeping an open mind about the possibility of a breakup has the benefit of preparing you to evaluate the relationship.

- Keeping an open mind about the possibility of a breakup means that you don't have to marry the other person at any cost. You know your value.

- Be courageous enough to breakup during the courtship if warranted, instead of grudgingly getting married only to divorce later.

- Keeping an open mind about the possibility of a breakup means you understand that a failed courtship is safer and better than a failed marriage.

- Be careful to remember that your decision to breakup is being made out of love and is going to be mutually beneficial in the long run.

- Be aware of the possibility that the other person may not understand your point of view and may accuse you of being selfish.

CHAPTER NINE

PROCEED WITH NO PLAN B IN MIND

> *Just as good marriages go bad, bad marriages go good. And they have a better chance of doing so in a society that recognizes the value of marriage than one that sings the statistically dubious joys of divorce.*
>
> *—Maggie Gallagher*

Buy now, and if you aren't completely satisfied, get your money back. Thanks to our postmodern retail world, we're encouraged to buy and try it out, and if we aren't completely satisfied then we can return the product and get a full refund. With some observable evidence around us, this marketing philosophy seems to be slowly creeping into the hallowed institution of marriage.

With the increasing frequency of divorce happening all around us, one can only interpret that to mean some people are saying, "Come now, babe. Let's try this out, and if it doesn't work out, we'll go our separate ways." That kind of mindset seems to be the response to a growing effort to trivialize marriage. Some marriage registries have in the recent past added drive-throughs as an option for marrying couples.

> *Come now, Babe. Let's try this out, and if it doesn't work out, we'll go our separate ways.*

For example, Niagara Falls Wedding Chapel offers interested Canadians the option of a drive-through wedding. There are also a couple of such drive-throughs in Las Vegas, USA. Their slogan is "Marriage through the fast lane." But I call it a "hamburger marriage!" Such a marriage practice begs the question of whether it has reduced marriage to be on the same level as buying a hamburger at a drive-through in a fast-food restaurant?

Perhaps, some who choose to marry via the drive through just want a simple wedding. I get that. But I think it is still possible to get married with a simple wedding that doesn't cost a lot of money without necessarily taking the route of the drive-through. For example, you can arrange with your pastor to have them join you in a quiet and simple ceremony. This can be held during a Sunday evening service or any day of the week for that matter. There are many possibilities.

It is important to build our understanding of marriage on the original principles upon which God founded it, and not on the understanding that's based on the philosophies of our constantly evolving world. I say this with a great sense of responsibility and respect for those many faithful believers who have suffered or are still suffering the pain of a separation or even divorce. I know some of these faithful and well-respected believers closely. To these people and those like them, I humbly say with all my heart, "I feel your pain."

Let me stress that if you're in a new marriage following the failure of your previous marriage or marriages, my position is not intended in any way to denigrate you and your new marriage. Absolutely not! I am only responding to what the Spirit of God has put in my heart regarding this thorny issue that the church is facing today. I am aware that there's a diversity of opinions on the issue of divorce, and mine is just one of many views.

The deep pain confessed by many who have gone through divorce goes to show that something is not right with it. I don't think it's difficult to see that a good thing shouldn't cause so much anguish to all those involved. It's not a surprise that people don't go into marriage with the aspiration to divorce and enter a new marriage. Very few people, if any, get married with the expectation that one day they will divorce.

The deep pain confessed by many who have gone through divorce goes to show that something is not right with it.

Divorce violates the foundational principle upon which God created marriage, and it breaks the trust that marriage is intended to be built upon. Some proponents of divorce have argued that although the hurt associated with it is real, it'll eventually go away. As a result, they propose that those who no longer feel like staying married to their partner should seek divorce without considering any other form of intervention.

It is with this conviction that I am suggesting that people should refrain from marrying until they understand what marriage is and prepare for it. Typically, it is those who go into marriage without a proper understanding of what it entails or what it takes to lead a successful married life that are quick to take the "Plan B" route. Plan B is to say to yourself that if it does not work, I will back out or divorce. In general, Plan B usually isn't anyone's best choice but it is the convenient way out of the situation. It cheapens the relationship, and it's the route that's typically taken by those who lack the tenacity to insist upon their first and best option. Your ultimate path should be the one that leads to your first choice, not the path to the second choice.

Not having a Plan B ensures that you'll give your marriage everything you've got to make it work from the point of making your "Go or No Go" decision. And it's important that such a decision is preceded by a meaningful and intentional courtship. If you get your courtship right, then excluding Plan B easily becomes the wise and natural choice.

Your due diligence during the courtship period ensures that you're going into marriage with no expectation of any major surprises. You know your intended spouse well enough to say with confidence, "They are the right person for me."

The Importance of Commitment

Many people have argued that they divorced or wanted a divorce because they no longer felt the same love they once felt for their spouse. They suggest that ending the marriage and starting a fresh and exciting relationship will give them greater happiness and contentment. But it is important to understand that marriage is much more than a feeling of love.

If the simplistic feeling of love is all that you're after, then you probably have some gaps in your understanding of what marriage really is. If your pursuit is a fresh and feel-good experience, then hopping from one partner to another may be your best bet.

The kind of love that is necessary to sustain a marriage has two important components—a decision and a commitment. A clear understanding of marriage as a lifetime undertaking means you *decide* that you are up to the task of getting married and is followed by an unwavering *commitment* that you will invest everything that you've to make it work.

Furthermore, commitment helps partners to see their relationship and their emotional bond as the most important thing in their lives. They stay married because they want to, not out of necessity or a sense of responsibility. The emotional aspect of commitment enhances our marriages because it directs how we feel about our spouse; how we feel about them regulates how we treat or relate to them.

Furthermore, couples who are committed to their partners tend to think of each other in a positive light. After all, how can we be emotionally committed to another person if we don't think favourably of them? Committed partners tend to work hard to keep their relationship strong, and in times of conflict they try their best to defuse the situation and bring it under control. Additionally, committed partners tend to sacrifice their personal needs and focus more on pursuing needs that serve the couple as a whole.

It is true that the starting point of a marital relationship is love. However, I will say that commitment is the most important prerequisite for an enduring marriage. An enduring marriage that spans a lifetime can be described this way: I have *decided* that I love you enough to marry you for as long as I live, and I am *committed* to loving you until death separates us! Ruth the Moabitess demonstrated this level of commitment to Naomi, her mother-in-law:

But Ruth said: "Entreat me not to leave you,
Or to turn back from following after you; For wherever you go, I will go; And wherever you lodge, I will lodge; Your people shall be my people, And your God, my God. Where you die, I will die, And there will I be buried. The Lord do so to me, and more also, If anything but death parts you and me." (Ruth 1:16-17 NKJV)

What a beautiful and kind-hearted woman! She loved her husband so much that even after he had passed away, she continued to be loyal and committed to his mother. If we show our unalloyed commitment to our marriage, there shouldn't be any problems arising that we'll not be able to overcome as a couple. When there's a wholehearted commitment to doing something, we normally will deploy everything that is needed to get that thing done. Commitment has a way of bringing worthy causes to a glorious end. The same is true of marriage.

A friend of mine once told me an intriguing story of a military commander who went to war with his soldiers. The commander and his troops came to a fast-flowing river. They quickly built a makeshift bridge and crossed over to fight the enemies. As common military tradition dictates, the soldiers crossed over and left their commander on the other side of the raging river. This is called commanding from the rear. At some point, the battle became so fierce that his troops were about to retreat.

> *Commitment has a way of bringing worthy causes to a glorious end.*

The commanding officer ordered his bodyguards to destroy the makeshift bridge to prevent his troops from retreating. He ordered his troops to stay and fight. The troops soon realized that only two difficult options were available to them; to stay and fight, and either defeat their enemies or retreat and be drowned in the raging river. They chose the lesser of the two evils. They stayed and put up a gallant fight until they won. Their commitment and resilience made the difference.

There is a parallel between this story and some marriages. Some of the challenges that couples face in a marriage are best described as being in the battlefield. But when they resolve to stay and put up a fight for their marriage, there's almost always a sweet victory in the end. Fighting for your marriage means working on your marriage, praying, and seeking wise counsel from those you consider to be more knowledgeable and more experienced than you. If for any reason you are still not successful, you'll be satisfied that at least you did all that you could to save your marriage.

Feeling Is Fleeting

As we all know so well, our feelings are transient. That's why feelings shouldn't be relied upon to sustain a marriage. Our feelings are most likely going to change because they are based on so many factors including environment, mood, prevailing circumstances, and so on. For that reason, there's absolutely no guarantee that your feelings about anything in life will be constant from day to day. The same is true of marriage. One may be setting themselves up for failure or at least for a rude shock should they be expecting their feelings toward their spouse to be constant.

A friend once told me a story about a pastor who was officiating a wedding. He admonished the couple with these words:

> *You've decided to spend the rest of your life together because of your feelings. But the rest of your life together will be decided by your actions. Take a good look at your hands, the pastor requested of the couple. Because it is what you do in the days, weeks, months, and years to come that'll determine what you'll see in each other's eyes. In other words, what you see is not what you get. What you do is what you see.*

Also, it's important for couples to realize that every relationship has cycles. Marital relationships are no exception. After some years of marriage, the euphoria of the feel-so-good love fades, at least it does occasionally. You don't have to take it personally; it's the natural and inevitable cycle of every relationship.

Every relationship exhibits the symptoms of this stage a little a bit differently. However, if you're thoughtful and observant about your marriage, you'll notice the difference between the initial stage of when you first fell in love and the subsequent stage when you simply don't feel the love anymore. The right response to this dilemma does not lie outside your marriage. It lies within it. For that reason, I will suggest that you shouldn't start looking for a Plan B. Instead, look inward and start looking for ways that will lubricate your marriage all over again.

It is also important to appreciate that there are specific things you can do with or without your spouse to make your marriage high-functioning as well as successful. Just as there are physical laws of nature, there are also laws or principles that ensure the success of marital relationships. Like the right diet and exercise routine makes you physically healthier and stronger, certain habits in your relationship will surely go a long way in making your marriage healthier, stronger, and long-lasting. It'd be safe to describe it as a garbage in and garbage out kind of undertaking. If you know and apply the principles, the results are predictable.

The comprehensive principles or laws that are necessary and sufficient for a successful marriage are contained in ***Volume* 2** of my ***Family Life Handbook*** series.

> *There are specific things you can do with or without your spouse to succeed in your marriage.*

KEY TAKE AWAY

- Marriage shouldn't be entered with a "Plan B" in mind. You should fully invest in your marriage with all your mind, soul, and spirit.
- Marriage is a lifelong undertaking; therefore, don't get married simply to try it out.
- Unless your motivation is to have a simple and cost-effective wedding, I think those who get married at the drive-through wedding chapels may be devaluing their marriage.
- Attractiveness and love begin in the first stages of a long-term marital relationship, but commitment is what will sustain it over the long-term.
- A strong correlation exists between the longevity of your marriage and the time and effort you put into it.
- What you see in your marriage is not what you get, but what you do is what you see. It is a garbage in and garbage out kind of undertaking.
- At any point in your marriage, what will make your marriage thrive lies within your marriage and not outside of it.

CHAPTER TEN

AN EPILOGUE

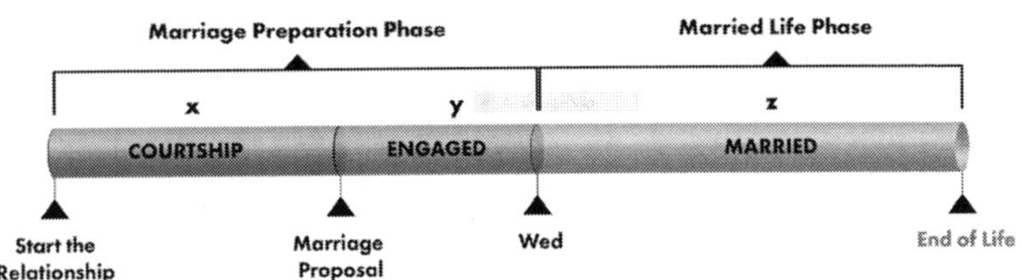

x = Should be long enough to know your selves well, but not too long to cause weariness.
y = Prepare for wedding. Should not be longer than 12 months.
z = should last until at least one of the spouses passes away.

Fig 1: Stages in the Marriage Process and Key Milestones

As you have read in the preceding pages, the picture above shows the phases and milestones that should follow in order within the marriage process. I truly hope you now understand why an intentional, goal-oriented courtship is important, why it should precede your marriage, and why it is needed to ensure your marriage relationship will continue to flourish over the long-term. I believe that beyond understanding you've also been impacted and inspired sufficiently to be able to act accordingly. As you step into the partnership of marriage, let me emphasize yet again that you've begun a journey of a lifetime because that's what marriage is. Developing such a mindset upfront is necessary for leading a successful married life.

Marriage is meant to be the most exciting and fun-filled relationship there is in your life. This is not wishful thinking, it can be your reality; however, you've a critical role to play in ensuring that you actually enjoy that reality. Consistent hard work and an unwavering dedication is required. And I've no doubt in my mind that you're determined to make your marriage an exemplary one to those around you. The more exemplary marriages there are, the more stable and peaceful world we'll all experience around us.

> *The more exemplary marriages there are, the more stable and peaceful world we'll all experience around us.*

A Prelude to Volume 2

As you begin your married life, you will want to read my next book, as building a wonderful and successful married life is the focus of ***Volume 2*** of my ***Family Life Handbook*** series. Here's a taste of what will be discussed and what you will learn:

- Understanding your responsibilities in the marriage and how best to devote your time and energy in living up to those responsibilities.

The husband must:

- ***Love your wife*** as much as Christ has loved the church. Christ's love for the church is both sacrificial and unconditional. The Bible instructs, "Husbands, love your wives, just as Christ also loved the church and gave Himself for her, that He might sanctify and cleanse her with the washing of water by the word, that He might present her to Himself a glorious church, not having spot or wrinkle or any such thing, but that she should be holy and without blemish." (Ephesians 5:25-27 NKJV)

- ***Nourish, provide,*** and ***care*** for your wife.
- Endeavour to provide ***effective leadership*** for her.

The wife must:

- ***Submit*** yourself to your husband.
- Be your husband's unwavering ***cheerleader.***

There are some responsibilities that both the husband and the wife share to ensure that their marriage will thrive and last a lifetime. I've called these "Areas of Mutual Responsibility." These include:

- ***Respecting*** each other.
- ***Prioritizing*** your marital relationship and placing it at the top of all other interpersonal relationships you both have.
- ***Supporting*** each other.
- ***Caring, providing*** and ***protecting*** each other.
- Understanding that marriage is a ***partnership*** like no other.
- Understanding the central role ***sexual intimacy*** plays in strengthening your marriage bond.
- Working together intentionally to ***bequeath legacies*** to your children.

Additionally, you must beware of some subtle things that act as lubricants in marriage. I've called them subtle because they're often overlooked by undiscerning couples. But when they're accorded the necessary priority, they smoothen the engine and balance the wheels that drive your marriage. These actions include:

- Make sure that you're always working in ***agreement***. Sometimes it may be necessary for you to bend over backwards to achieve agreement in your marriage. But don't hesitate to do the work because your marriage is worth it.
- Race to see who will be the first to ***apologize***. Don't waste anytime to put any grievances behind you. Make sure the apology is genuine and straight from the heart. Be quick to forgive and let go of the offence.
- Let your spouse be always ***enough*** for you. Let them always be all you need as an intimate partner. For the husband, never fail to remember that as she has children with you, her physical body may change, but she remains your wife and the love of your life.
- Seek and retain a wise and godly ***counsellor***. You'll need counsellors to help you navigate differences or even conflicts in your marriage. This is not letting outsiders into your marital life, neither does it mean you're stupid and incapable of resolving your differences. But if a conflict persists and is impacting your inner peace or your marriage, you'll be well-advised to reach out to your trusted counsellor.

Always remember that for a Christian, marriage is for a lifetime. Therefore, never let the thought of divorce ever cross your mind. You must know ahead of time that there could be conflict between you and your spouse. But you must also never forget that with God at the centre of your marriage, any conflict can be satisfactorily resolved. That's why divorce should never be an option. Divorce is not good! Thus, I've taken the time to detail in *Volume 2* the ills of divorce from the biblical standpoint. Additionally, I've described the impact of divorce on the couple and society in general, and why building a solid marriage is so important.

Finally, as divorce has become the reality of many in our world today, I've closed volume 2 with words of hope and encouragement for those who may have divorced. I've provided tools to help them overcome the hurt that's often associated with divorce. In addition, as children are commonly cut up in the middle of many divorce cases, I've provided supporting content to help single mothers to more effectively navigate their new role.

REFERENCES

1 Young, K. (2006, July 19). Money advice and Banking Tips. Lifehack. Retrieved September 22, 2021, from http://www.lifehack.org/arcticles/money.

2 Waite, Linda & Gallagher, Maggie. (2000). The Case for Marriage. Contemporary Sociology. 30. 10.2307/3088984.